Successful Information Processing

Successful Information Processing

A coursebook for CLAIT and NVQ

Mary P. Jones

Stanley Thornes (Publishers) Ltd

First published in 1992 by:
Stanley Thornes (Publishers) Ltd
Old Station Drive
Leckhampton
CHELTENHAM   GL53 0DN
England

British Library Cataloguing in Publication Data

A catalogue record for this book is available from the British Library

ISBN 07487 1401 4

Typeset by Tech-Set, Gateshead, Tyne & Wear.
Printed and bound in Great Britain at The Bath Press, Avon.

CONTENTS

INTRODUCTION

In all spheres of society you will see or hear computers work. Computers are versatile, powerful and are the tools behind the Information Technology revolution. Information Technology covers all areas in which computers are used, and this book is designed to help you understand how they are used in industry and commerce and at the same time help prepare you for educational qualifications.

This book is mainly concerned with the three most common applications of computing included in the National Vocational Qualifications of NVQ Levels 1 and 2, Data Processing and Information Processing, namely Word Processing, Databases and Spreadsheets. In order to help you understand the full impact of Information Technology and meet the CLAIT syllabus it is also necessary to give you an overview of other computer applications.

By following the graded exercises you can gain the necessary skills to prepare yourself for NVQ assessment at Levels 1 and 2 for all examining boards.

You can also prepare yourself and test your skill for assessment for RSA Computer Literacy and Information Technology (CLAIT) Stage 1 with practice assignments. There is a skills checklist at the end of each application which enables you to check your progress.

How to use this book

Work through the sections in any order you wish. At certain points in the text you will be told when you have covered enough skills for a specific assessment. You can check your skills against the required criteria, then go to the assessment section and work through a practice assignment. Alternatively, continue through the exercises to further develop your skills, leaving the assessment checklist and assignments until the end.

Foreword

Successful Information Processing is intended as a students' workbook to be used with little tutor support. The exercises are not machine specific and may be used with any computer system or application. However, it is recommended that tutors check that exercises are compatible with the hardware/software used at their centres and that their students are familiar with terms used.

The book has been designed to meet the requirements for NVQ Units 3 – Data Processing, Unit 13 – Information Processing and RSA CLAIT Stage 1. The author deals mainly with the three most common computer applications of Word Processing, Spreadsheets and Databases included in the NVQ units, but has also included a very basic introduction to other areas applicable to the RSA CLAIT 1 Scheme. In addition, since the BTEC First Award Course is NVQ accredited, both the graded exercises and practice assignments are also applicable for that course. Furthermore, to complement the BTEC philosophy of integrating units, a section of integrated assignments has been included.

Exercises are graded in difficulty with help points throughout. These are included mainly as a guide to what is required, although it must be stressed that instructions are of a general nature and not specific instructions on how to use the system.

NVQs are competence based and after building their skills students can check their progress and practice an assignment before actually putting themselves forward for assessment. Alternatively, the practice assignments can be adapted for use as assessment material.

Courses for which the book is suitable include RSA and LCCI Business Administration or, indeed, any NVQ accredited course, BTEC First Award, CLAIT courses, or any other course in Information Technology. It is hoped that any Lecturer teaching Information Technology will find *Successful Information Processing* useful, either as a course book or as a source of material to dip into in order to supplement their own material.

ACKNOWLEDGEMENTS

The author and publisher are grateful to the following who have given permission to reproduce material:

The BBC, The Independent Broadcasting Authority and British Telecommunications.

The author also wishes to acknowledge her husband Alan, for his continued patience, support and determined mastery of IT applications and for painstakingly working through the graded exercises and assignments. Grateful thanks are made to colleagues, Roy Crane, Bob Larcombe, Geraldine Hannam and Paul Scrivens with particular thanks to colleagues Vivienne Edwards and Andy Gatehouse for their help in piloting exercises, checking and proof reading and to Mary James of Stanley Thornes (Publishers) Ltd for her belief in the book.

PART 1
SKILLS BUILDING

MODULE 1

WORD PROCESSING

Introduction

'Word processing' is the term given to the processing of text using a computer. The primary advantage is that text can be keyed in on an electronic keyboard, viewed on a screen and corrected before being printed. Text can also be saved on to disk and recalled at a later date for further additions or corrections to be made. The work is then updated and the new version stored. When additions or corrections are made, the text is reshuffled back within its margins either automatically on sophisticated systems or by the *reformat* command on smaller packages.

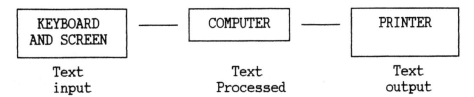

Figure 1   An illustration of a basic stand-alone system

Word processing has provided a major breakthrough for the typist by taking all the hard work out of typewriting, with, for example, its automatic centring of text, emboldening and a host of other facilities. No longer does the typist have to consider retyping an unsatisfactory document because major changes such as transferring large portions of text from one page to another and reshuffling (reformatting) text within the margins can be easily undertaken. There is also no need for the typist to press the carriage return at the end of a line because the word processor automatically calculates how much room there is for a word and wraps the remaining text around to the next line. This is known as *wraparound.*

There are two types of word processor, a *dedicated* system which can only be used for word processing or a *menu-driven* system which is normally a package that can be used on a computer capable of other applications. Word processors can also be part of an integrated package.

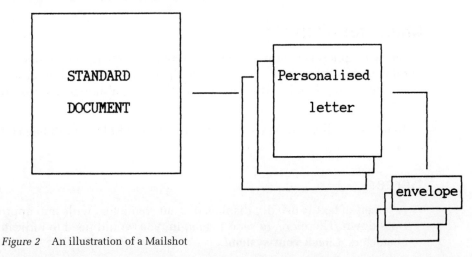

Figure 2   An illustration of a Mailshot

3

There are numerous applications for which word processing is suitable, one of which is *Mailshot,* whereby a standard letter can be typed and stored, and then merged with another document containing addresses to produce a personalised letter for each person or organisation in the address file.

In order to help you word process for business, here is some information on layout and display techniques.

Page set up

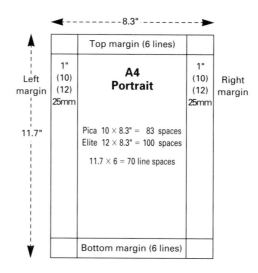

In order to set up a page it is necessary to understand page specifications.

Top margin — This is a number of lines which are left before text is printed on the page. Most word processors have a default top margin, i.e. automatically set within the program.

Bottom margin — A number of lines left after the end of text on a page but before the bottom of the paper. Most word processors have a default bottom margin.

Left margin — Some word processors have a default left margin, i.e. an automatic offset from the left-hand side of the paper.

Right margin — Some word processors have a default right hand margin.

Some word processors need to have the page set up before a document is typed whilst others have a default page set up.

Paper sizes are international and the most commonly used is A4 (as shown above). A4 is half A3 whilst A5 is half of A4. There are also other sizes. If the paper is used with the shorter edge to the top, it is called portrait but if it is used with the longer edge at the top, it is called landscape.

Character pitch

Character pitch is a term given to the number of characters to one inch, hence 12 pitch means there are 12 characters to the inch. Most word processors have a default of 10 pitch, i.e. 10 characters to the inch, although some allow a change of pitch.

10 pitch is called PICA whilst 12 pitch is called ELITE. Both have 6 lines to the inch.

Screen

A screen of text is usually displayed as 80 characters wide and approximately 25 lines down. Therefore, to set a 1" margin, you would need to indicate 10 characters. **Check your system!**

Some word processors use different units of measurement to calculate page widths, lengths and pitch. Some use inches whilst others use the number of characters per inch. Some use other units of measurement such as millimetres. Before setting margins for the word processing exercises you will need to familiarise yourself with your particular system and find out how to calculate margin spaces. Instructions will be given in inches.

Business documentation

The layout of a business letter (fully blocked with open punctuation) is shown below.

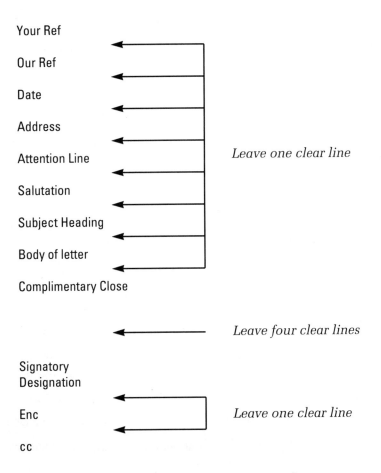

Your Ref

Our Ref

Date

Address

Attention Line   *Leave one clear line*

Salutation

Subject Heading

Body of letter

Complimentary Close

                                  Leave four clear lines

Signatory
Designation

Enc   *Leave one clear line*

cc

Memoranda

A *memorandum* is used for internal communication between one person and another within the same organisation. The two alternatives are shown below. It is important that you are consistent with spacing, leaving two spaces before infilling information and/or aligning infill information.

MEMORANDUM   MEMORANDUM

From   Ted Royston   From   Mr Royston

To   Julia Filshey   To   Miss Filshey

Date   23 May 1992   Date   23 May 1992

The reference (if required) appears at the left margin, two clear line spaces after the body of the memorandum, e.g. Ref. ABC/123.

Proofreading

Proofreading is the term used to describe the action of checking typewritten or word processed work for errors. There are a number of different errors which might occur:

Spelling errors	Words spelled incorrectly
Typographical errors	Words or characters not typed correctly or typed in incorrect order, inserted or omitted
	Capitals used instead of lower case characters or vice versa
	Inconsistency in use of upper or lower case characters
Spacing errors	Spacing between words, sentences, lines or paragraphs
Punctuation	Incorrect punctuation or omission of punctuation
Grammatical errors	Errors in grammar of words/sentences.

Hints on proofreading

When proofreading a document, always check for all types of errors. It is good practice to use a ruler to guide one's eye across a page or trace each word and space with a finger while reading from original copy. If your system has the facility to display spaces with dots, switch it on before proof reading from the screen.

Correction signs

When changes or corrections have to be made to typewritten or handwritten work, the author or proofreader uses signs which are understood by all involved in the processing of text. Correction signs are normally placed in the margin on the same line as the text to be changed and sometimes another sign is inserted in the actual text.

Signs in margin	Meaning	Signs in text
lc/	Lower case character required	_ under letter
uc /or CAPS	Upper case character required type the word(s) in capital letters	= under letter(s) ≡ or under word(s)
ꝏ	Delete or take out	/ through letter/word
NP or //	New paragraph	[before first word
stet	Let it stand, i.e. as original type word with _ _ _ _ _ under the crossed out word	...... under word(s)
run on	No new paragraph required – carry straight on – join paragraph	⌇
⋏	This sign is a *caret,* and means insert letter or word(s)	⋏ placed where text is to be added
⌣	Close up – less space required	⌣ between letter/word
trs/	Transpose, i.e. change order of letters or words	∿ between letters or words (sometimes numbered)
#	Insert space	#
FILIGREE	If a word is not clear in the text, it may be written in the margin in capitals and enclosed in a box, although it must be typed in the text as normal	

Word Processing

Word Processing   Exercise 1

SKILL BUILDING towards
NEW CLAIT 1.1, 1.4
NVQ I Unit 3 Element 3.1

Learning Point   Creating a document
Keying in text
Saving a document
Printing a document

Task 1   Key in the following text and print one copy. Save your document onto disk using an appropriate filename for use in another exercise.

FIRST IMPRESSIONS

First impressions are very important and could be the basis on which a person reacts to another person possibly for the rest of their lives. A 'good impression' is something that is open to varied interpretation. For example, it is assumed when attending a job interview for an office job that creating a 'good impression' means being dressed suitably for work in an office. It also means being prompt for the interview and presenting an efficient image.

7

Word Processing   Exercise 2

Learning Point   Creating a document
Keying in text
Saving a document
Printing a document

Task 1   Key in the following text and print one copy. Save your document.

FINDING A JOB

This is easier said than done in these days of economic restraint. Find out on which day jobs are advertised in your local newspaper and check weekly to find vacancies. The Department of Employment runs a service which is known as a Jobcentre. There is one in most towns and cities. If you are still at school pay a visit to your School Careers Officer. There are also private employment agencies such as Kelly Girl or The Brook Street Bureau. These types of agencies maintain a register of office workers and put applicants in touch with firms looking for employees. The agency charges employers a fee and very often the applicant works under contract to the agency.

Having found a vacancy, the next thing is to send for details. Some vacancies offer details and give a name and address to which to write - others have a telephone number to ring. Sometimes a box number will be given in place of a firm's name and this makes it difficult for an applicant to know to whom he/she is writing. Firms use a box number to maintain privacy and prevent casual callers at their premises. Some firms respond with an application form, others request a letter of application together with a curriculum vitae.

Word Processing   Exercise 3

Learning Point   Recalling a document
Editing text
Adding further text
Resaving document
Printing a document

Task 1   Recall the document you created in Exercise 1 and edit as follows.

FIRST IMPRESSIONS

First impressions are ~~very~~ *so* important and could *possibly* be the basis
on which a person reacts to another person ~~possibly~~ for the
rest of their lives. A 'good impression' is something that
is open to varied interpretation. For example, it is
assumed when attending a job interview for an office job
that creating a 'good impression' means being dressed
suitably for work in an office. It also means being prompt
for the interview and presenting an efficient image.

Task 2   Add the following text, resave and print your document.

NP // Creating a 'good impression' is particularly important in a
job interview because the interviewer has very little time
to decide on your merits. He/she has your letter of
application and possibly a curriculum vitae giving a ~~resume~~ *list*
of your qualifications for the job but interviewers need a
little more than that to warrant a job offer and it is at
time this ~~point~~ that first impressions are essential. To clinch
the job, be prompt, be neatly dressed, adopt a clear,
concise, well-spoken attitude and be enthusiastic.

Word Processing   Exercise 4

Learning Point   Recalling a document
Editing text
Resaving document
Printing a document

Task 1   Recall the document you created in Exercise 2, make the corrections as shown, resave and print one copy.

FINDING A JOB

recession

This is easier said than done in these days of economic ~~restraint~~. Find out on which day jobs are advertised in your local newspaper and check weekly to find vacancies. The Department of Employment runs ~~a service which is known as a~~ Jobcentre/ There is one in most towns and cities. If you are still/ ~~at school~~ pay a visit to your School Careers Officer. There are also private employment agencies such as Kelly Girl or The Brook Street Bureau. These types of agencies maintain a register of office workers and put applicants in touch with firms looking for employees. The agency/ charges/ employers a fee and very often the applicant works under contract to the agency.

s
a student

uc / ies

further information

Having found a vacancy, the next thing is to send for ~~details~~. Some ~~vacancies~~ offer details and give a name and *companies* address to which to write - others have a telephone number to ring. Sometimes a box number will be given in place of a firm's name and this makes it difficult for an applicant to know to whom he/she is writing. Firms use a box number to maintain privacy and prevent casual callers at their premises. Some firms respond with an application form, others request a letter of application/together with a curriculum vitae.   *in your own handwriting*

Word Processing   Exercise 5

Learning Point   Creating a document
Keying in text
Centring text
Printing a document

Task 1   Key in the following text, centring every line and print one copy.

Help Point   To centre means to position text in the middle of a line on the screen. Word processors have a facility for this. Refer to your system guide to operate this facility.

```
                    SITUATIONS VACANT


                ANGLO-FRENCH CONNECTION



                        require
                  A Personal Assistant
              to work in a busy city office


                     He/she must be

                  A fast accurate typist
                Able to work under pressure
                 Able to work in a team
                    Fluent in French


      A knowledge of Importing and Exporting would be an asset


           Apply initially in own handwriting for details
```

Word Processing   Exercise 6

Learning Point   Creating a document
Keying in text
Centring text
Emboldening text
Printing a document

Task 1   Key in the following text, centring every line and emboldening marked words. Print a copy.

Before You Start   To embolden text means to overprint it several times to make it stand out. This is a word processing facility. Refer to your system guide to operate this facility.

```
CONFERENCE CENTRE FOR M4 CORRIDOR - MIDLAND LINK

THE WYE & SEVERN MOTEL
ST ARVANE
CHEPSTOW
GWENT
NP2 7MW

Tel 0291 675/283/621   BOLD
Telex 4219506


*  *  *  *  *


TARIFF
Inclusive of Full Welsh Breakfast

Per Person per night including VAT @ 17.5%

Weekday Monday - Thursday £32.50
Weekend Friday - Sunday £28.50

Facilities for 200 delegates   BOLD
Conference Rates available at Reception
```

Word Processing   Exercise 7

Learning Point   Creating a document
Setting margins
Keying in text
Centring text
Emboldening text
Underscoring text
Printing a document

Task 1   Key in the following text, enhancing text as indicated, and print one copy.

Before You Start   Spaced captions means 1 space between each letter and 3 spaces between each word. Check your system notes on how to underscore (draw a line under text).

[CENTRE EVERY LINE — handwritten annotation]

THE WYE & SEVERN MOTEL — *SPACED CAPS AND BOLD*

CONFERENCE MENU — *BOLD*

Starters — *UNDERSCORE*

Salmon Mousse
Prawn Cocktail
Avocado Anne-Marie

Main Course — *UNDERSCORE*

Fresh Wye Salmon
Roast Duckling with orange sauce
Forest Nut Loaf

Seasonal Vegetables

Dessert — *UNDERSCORE*

Fresh Fruit Salad
Bombe Alaska
Trifle Angharad

Coffee and Truffles

[1" Margins — handwritten annotation]

The restaurant is open between 8 pm - 10 pm. Coffee may be taken in the Llandogo Lounge where there is a licensed bar open until midnight.

Word Processing   Exercise 8

Learning Point   Creating a document
Setting margins
Keying in text
Changing line length of paragraphs
Justifying/unjustifying right-hand margin
Printing a document

Task 1   Key in the following text using margins as follows:

Before You Start   Type Paragraph 1 with 1" margins
2 with 1.5" margins
3 with 2" margins
Check your system guide for instructions on how to do this.

A GLIMPSE OF MEDIEVAL PARIS

Ile Saint-Louis and its neighbour island, Ile de la Cité, provide one of the loveliest starting points for a tour of Paris. Both islands are bordered by peaceful, tree-lined quays and each offer visiting walkers superb views of beautiful avenues along with some of the capital's oldest monuments.

Charming, aristocratic Ile Saint-Louis is like a little urban jewel, casting tantalising images into the river Seine and is studded with elegant seventeenth-century mansions like a necklace of so many architectural pearls.

The Ile de la Cité is both the geographical and historic heart of Paris. Distances to and from Paris are measured from Notre-Dame, and it was on this island, and nearby Montagne Sainte-Genevieve, that the Gallo-Romans built the city they called Lutetia in the first century AD.

Task 2   Print two copies, one with a ragged right-hand margin and the second with a justified right-hand margin.

Before You Start   Justification means all text is flush (straight) at the right margin. Check your system guide to operate this word processing facility.

Word Processing   Exercise 9

Learning Point   Creating a document
Setting margins
Keying in text
Changing line length for inset paragraphs
Justifying right-hand margin
Changing line spacing
Printing a document

Task 1   Key in the following text using 1" margins and print one copy.

Before You Start   Use system settings remembering that the system will wraparound text at line endings.

BRUSSELS

The charm of the city is an acknowledged fact with its royal palaces and seventeenth-century guild houses. Time is needed to stroll around the beautiful squares taking in shopping or relaxing in a sidewalk cafe. No stay in Brussels is complete without visiting the Statue of 'Manneken Pis' or the Atomium.

BRUGES

When you visit Bruges you step back in time as you explore this medieval city with its narrow streets and canals. You can explore Bruges by foot or take a trip by boat. See traditional lace-makers at work, sample a waffle or sample famous Belgian chocolates. This mysterious city is a living museum with a wealth of art.

BARCELONA

Olympics 1992 - Barcelona your host. A special city which blends fiery excitement with Spanish tradition. It is cosmopolitan, international and has a superb artistic tradition. Climb the myriad of steps above the fountains after dark and gaze out on the exciting panoramic views of this splendid city.

Task 2   Inset 2nd and 3rd paragraphs as indicated below and print a further copy in double line spacing with justified margins.

- Keep paragraph 1 margins 1"
- Paragraph 2 margins 1.5"
- Paragraph 3 margins 2"

Word Processing   Exercise 10

Learning Point   Creating a document
Setting margins
Setting tabs
Printing a document

Task 1   Key in the following text with a ragged right-hand margin, indenting the first line of each paragraph. Print one copy.

Before You Start   To set a tab means to indicate a column you want text to begin at, usually a number of spaces in from the left margin. Check your system guide for instructions on how to do this.

WOMEN RETURNERS

A directory of Education and Training specifically aimed at women was published in May 1987. It was intended as a guide for all women irrespective of their educational background who were looking for courses to help them prepare to return to work or study.

This information was not previously available nationally either to Women Returners or anyone wishing to advise them. Because of this, some places on courses were unfilled possibly through poor publicity.

The directory has since been updated and course providers are being asked to give details of their courses so that in future equal opportunities will exist for all.

Colleges and training agencies are responding to this hitherto untapped workforce and are providing comprehensive training packages, including creche facilities.

Word Processing Exercise 11

Learning Point   Recalling a document
Editing text
Emboldening text
Joining paragraphs
Justifying text
Changing line spacing
Printing a document

Task 1   Recall the document you created in Exercise 10 and make the following corrections: embolden the heading, join the paragraphs as shown and justify the right-hand margin. Print one copy in double line spacing.

WOMEN RETURNERS

A directory of Education and Training specifically aimed at women was published in May 1987. It was intended as a guide for all women irrespective of their educational background who were looking for courses to help them prepare to return to work or study. *run on*

This information was not previously available nationally either to Women Returners or anyone wishing to advise them. Because of this, some places on courses were unfilled possibly through poor publicity. *run on*

The directory has since been updated and course providers are being asked to give details of their courses so that in future equal opportunities will exist for all. *run on*

Colleges and Training Agencies are responding to this hitherto untapped workforce and are providing comprehensive training packages, including creche facilities.

Word Processing   Exercise 12

Learning Point   Creating a document
Setting margins
Keying in text
Practising layout of memorandum (refer to word processing
  theory section)
Printing a document

Task 1   Key in the following text with $1\frac{1}{2}$" margins and a ragged right edge. Print a
copy. Save your document for use in another exercise.

MEMORANDUM

From   In-service training

To   Branch Managers

Date   Today's

ARRANGING A MEETING

Almost all businesses need to conduct meetings whether they
are formal Board of Director meetings, departmental
meetings or casual meetings between colleagues. Follow the
points below to organise a successful meeting.

Be clear in your own mind why you want a meeting and whom
you wish to attend. Ensure the time and venue of the
meeting is suitable for those you invite and double-check
booking arrangements of the room to be used. Before the
meeting, issue a notice giving the time and place and
include an agenda listing points to be discussed. If the
meeting is to take some time, arrange for refreshments and
ensure that all telephone calls are diverted to avoid
unnecessary interruptions. Finally, check all necessary
papers, writing materials and seating arrangements are in
order and you can look forward to an orderly start to your
meeting.

Word Processing   Exercise 13

Learning Point   Recalling a document
Splitting paragraphs
Inserting tabs into existing text
Printing a document

Task 1   Recall the exercise you created in Exercise 12 and make the following corrections.

Split each paragraph where indicated, and indent the first line of each new paragraph.

Help Point   Refer to your system guide for information on how to insert tabs.

MEMORANDUM

From   In-service training

To   Branch Managers

Date   Today's

ARRANGING A MEETING

Almost all businesses need to conduct meetings whether they are formal Board of Director meetings, departmental meetings or casual meetings between colleagues. Follow the points below to organise a successful meeting.

Be clear in your own mind why you want a meeting and whom
NP you wish to attend. [Ensure the time and venue of the meeting is suitable for those you invite and double-check
NP booking arrangements of the room to be used. [Before the meeting, issue a notice giving the time and place and
NP include an agenda listing points to be discussed. [If the meeting is to take some time, arrange for refreshments and ensure that all telephone calls are diverted to avoid
NP unnecessary interruptions. [Finally, check all necessary papers, writing materials and seating arrangements are in order and you can look forward to an orderly start to your meeting.

Word Processing   Exercise 14

Learning Point   Creating a document
Setting margins
Keying in text
Saving and recalling a document
Adding text
Printing

Task 1   Key in the following text with a ragged right-hand margin, using margins to equal 1" and print out a copy.

WATERING YOUR PLANTS

Unfortunately one of the most common causes of plant death is watering incorrectly. You can kill a plant with too much water just as you can with too little. Plants are made up of about 90% water, which they lose through their leaves. The water is replaced by being drawn up through the roots from the soil. If the soil is allowed to dry out, the plant is deprived of a source of water and eventually it will die.

Initial signs that all is not well is the wilting of the leaves. However, too much water will cause the same problem and also the leaves will turn yellow. This happens because water contains oxygen and if a constant supply is given to the soil, the oxygen already present is displaced and the roots suffocate to death and are unable to supply water to the stem and leaves.

Your plants do not like to be given cold water. Tepid water is fine and many people have a container of water at room temperature and use it only for their plants.

Task 2   Recall your document, insert the following to appear as the third paragraph and resave your document.

The technique of watering is very simple. You just pour the water gently until it reaches the top of the pot. It will very gently seep through the soil and any surplus water will drain away. Alternatively you can water from below by pouring water into the pot tray. Always check the soil and if it feels fairly moist then leave well alone.

Word Processing   Exercise 15

Learning Point   Recalling and editing a document
Changing the line spacing
Changing the line length to inset paragraph
Printing a document

Task 1   Correct as indicated and print your document.

WATERING YOUR PLANTS

incorrect
Unfortunately one of the most common causes of plant death
is watering incorrectly. You can kill a plant with too much
water just as you can with too little. Plants are made up
approx
stet
of about 90% water, which they lose through their leaves.
The water is replaced by being drawn up through the roots
from the soil. If the soil is allowed to dry out, the plant
is deprived of a source of water and eventually it will
die.

DOUBLE SPACING
Initial signs that all is not well is the wilting of the
leaves. However, too much water will cause the same problem
and also the leaves will turn yellow. This happens because
water contains oxygen and if a constant supply is given to
the soil, the oxygen already present is displaced and the
roots suffocate to death and are unable to supply water to
the stem and leaves.   *easy to pick up*

The technique of watering is very simple. You just pour the
water gently until it reaches the top of the pot. It will
very gently seep through the soil and any surplus water
will drain**s** away. Alternatively you can water from below by
pouring water into the pot tray. Always check the soil   **uc**
regularly
and if it feels fairly moist then leave well alone.

change line length to inset paragraph ½" from each margin
Your plants do not like to be given cold water. Tepid water
is fine and many people have a container of water at room
temperature and use it only for their plants.

You will have now covered all the word processing functions necessary for RSA CLAIT Word Processing. You have two options:

1   If you already have typing skills and feel ready to tackle an assignment, check your skills against the CLAIT Checklist on page 47, then turn to the CLAIT Word Processing Assignments on page 176.

2   Continue with the exercises, which will give further practice in keying in, until you feel more confident.

Task 2   Centre the heading, change the order of the last two paragraphs and print your document.

21

Word Processing Exercise 16

Learning Point Creating a document
Setting margins and tabs
Printing a document

Task 1 Key in the following text, and print one copy. Use appropriate margins and tabs.

```
FLIGHT DETAILS

Depart          Nights    Dep Time      Ret Time      Holiday
Gatwick to                                            Number

Venice          7         Sun 1310      Sun 1945      LGVE01

Florence        7         Sun 1445      Sun 1940      LGFL06

Moscow          7         Fri 1410      Fri 2210      LGMO40

Cairo           14        Thu 1515      Thu 1100      LGCA59

New York        21        Fri 1410      Fri 0600      LGNY41
```

Word Processing   Exercise 17

Learning Point   Creating a document
Setting margins and tabs
Consolidating layout of memorandum
Printing a document

Task 1   Key in the following text, setting tabs to ensure five spaces between columns, and print one copy.

MEMORANDUM

From   Sales Manager

To   Advertising

Date   Today's

FRENAMEN CLOTHES PEG

The following sizes are to be included in the fashion review article, scheduled for publication in our January 92 issue:

FRENCH, ENGLISH AND US CLOTHING SIZES

Women's dresses and blouses
Robes et tricots femme

France	36	38	40	42	44	46	48
GB	10	12	14	16	18	20	22
USA	8	10	12	14	16	18	20

Men's suits
Costumes hommes

France	36	38	40	42	44	46	48
GB	35	36	37	38	39	40	42
USA	35	36	37	38	39	40	42

Word Processing   Exercise 18

Learning Point   Creating a document
Keying in text from manuscript
Consolidating memoranda layout
Printing a document

Task 1   Key in the following text using 1" margins and print one copy.

MEMORANDUM   (Today's date)

From Personnel officer

To   All Staff

SICK LEAVE PROCEDURES

All staff should endeavour to let inform their immediate superior of impending leave ie visits to Dr, Dentist or sickness. Where poss. before 9.00 AM on day in question.

After two days staff should complete a self certification form and after one week a Dr's certificate will be required.

Word Processing   Exercise 19

Learning Point   Creating a document
Setting margins and tabs
Keying in text
Practising memoranda layout
Printing a document

Task 1   Key in the following memo using 1" margins and print one copy.

MEMORANDUM

From   Managing Director

To   Sales Manager

Date   12 November 1991

Further to our conversation prior to the Board Meeting on Wednesday last, the end of year figures for our Paris office are as follows:

	1990	1991
Turnover	12 557	15 859
Pre-tax profit	3 596	4 697
Earnings per ordinary share	15.035p	18.569p
Total net dividend per ordinary share	3.9130p	4.9567p

The year 1991 is the third successive year that we have achieved an increase in turnover.

These figures are higher than we had anticipated and indicate an upward trend in our European market. You should endeavour to visit our Paris office at the earliest possible time to deliver our long-term project plan to your French sales counterpart.

Keep me informed of all progress over the next few months.

Word Processing   Exercise 20

Learning Point Creating a document
Setting margins and tabs
Keying in text
Practising layout of business letter
Printing a document

Task 1   Key in the following letter and print one copy.

Before You Start   Set 1" margins and set tabs for columns with five spaces between

```
                              LIFESURE
                      26 King Charles Square
                              CARDIFF
                              CF1 2KT

Our Ref CH/JR/DD/014

12 May 1990

Mrs M P Taylor
15 The Hawthorns
Llantwit Major
Nr Barry
South Glamorgan
BA8 7PP


Dear Mrs Taylor

In accordance with the regulations incorporated in the
Open Direct Debiting Mandate system we are required to
provide you with advance notice of the first request
under a mandate or the first request following a change
in your bank details.

The amount of £95 detailed below will be debited from
the above account within the next few days.

Policy Number        Name              Premium

43765434T            Taylor M P        95 regular monthly

Yours faithfully
LIFESURE




D H SHARMA
Premium Department
```

Word Processing   Exercise 21

Learning Point   Creating a document
Setting margins and tabs
Keying in text
Consolidating letter layout
Printing a document

Task 1   Key in the following letter, using suitable margins, with a justified right-hand margin, and print a copy.

```
Your Ref FJL/CO

Our Ref  MPJ/AJ

Today's date

FOR THE ATTENTION OF MR F J LAYCOCK


Bilsdon Motors Ltd
23 Queen Street
ST ALBANS
Herts
HE1 8TN


Dear Sirs

BULK PURCHASING

In reply to your letter of the 4 September, we have
pleasure in quoting the following prices:

30     Windscreen Wiper Blades     WB234     £13.60 each
40     Seat Covers                 SC125     £9.25 each
25     Cassette Cases              CA30      £4.95 each

Our area representative will be calling at your
premises during the next few days and will be pleased
to deliver your order then. Please confirm by writing
if you wish to be supplied with the above.


Yours faithfully
THAMESIDE MOTOR CO LTD




DAVID CAWLEY
SALES MANAGER
```

Word Processing   Exercise 22

**SKILL BUILDING towards
NVQ I Unit 3 Element 3.1**

Learning Point   Creating a document
Setting margins and tabs
Practising for assessment in NVQ Unit 3 Element 3.1
Producing a letter, memorandum and envelope
Printing documents

Task 1   Key in the following text using suitable margins, and print one copy.

```
Our Ref DK/YI

Today's date

Mrs F Twining
31 The Maze
TETBURY
Glos
GL29 TE3

Dear Mrs Twining

COOKRITE KITCHENS

Further to your request for details of our extensive
range of fitted kitchens, we have pleasure in
specifying our service and quoting our figures as
follows:

Every COOKRITE kitchen is an investment, designed and
built to your individual requirements and our high
specification and standards.

Our specialists will be pleased to call and give a free
survey of your kitchen. We have a computerised planning
service which can take your ideas and turn them into
workable templates and give a costing at the same time.

CALIFORNIA      White melamine finish      £1153.00
FLORIDA         Light oak finish           £2035.50
ALCUDIA         Mahogany finish            £4860.00
CALGARY         Red cedar                  £5020.00

We look forward to hearing from you in the near future.


Yours sincerely
COOKRITE KITCHENS




Lester Cartwright
Sales Executive
```

Task 2   Type an envelope for the letter on page 28.

Before You Start   Study the envelope shown below and note the following points:

- The address should start at approximately half-way down the envelope and approximately one-third from the left edge.
- Each part of the address should start on a new line.
- The town should be typed in capital letters.
- The postcode should be typed in capital letters with one space between its two parts.

```
Mrs F Twining
31 The Maze
TETBURY
Glos
GL29 TE3
```

Figure 3   Addressing an envelope

Word Processing   Exercise 23

Learning Point Creating a document
Producing a letter within a 10 minute period, leading towards
competence in NVQ Unit 3 Element 3.1
Printing a document

Task 1 Key in the following letter, choose appropriate margins, and print one
copy. Produce an envelope.

```
                    SWAYNE & BELLING
                     Estate Agents
                      Marine Walk
                    TENBY TH1 3MA

Telephone 0459 67823                Fax 0459 69876

Our Ref BJE/NEM/08

Today's date

Mr & Mrs T Somerville
Karenza
Sea View Close
TENBY
Dyfed  TH1 3MW

Dear Mr & Mrs Somerville

KARENZA, SEA VIEW CLOSE, TENBY, DYFED

I am writing to acknowledge your kind instructions for
this firm to act as selling agents on your behalf,
offering the above property for sale by private treaty
at an asking price of £56,000. Our charges for selling
property on a sole agency basis are calculated as
commission of 1.3% of the sale price plus VAT at 17.5%.
This is inclusive of advertising.

We shall arrange for advertisements to appear in the
local press and a 'For Sale' sign to be erected at the
front of your property. As and when prospective
purchases wish to view, we shall make mutually
convenient arrangements with you. Finally, may we take
this opportunity to thank you for your kind
instructions in this matter.


Yours sincerely


Ms E Dowding
SWAYNE & BELLING
```

Word Processing   Exercise 24

Learning Point Creating a document
Keying in text from manuscript
Consolidating memoranda layout
Printing a document

MEMORANDUM

From   David Simpson ((Co-ordinator)

To   WP Engineer

Date   Today's   *Be consistent with layout*

See Secretarial Services   (CAPS)

Will you please visit the above company at 2 Beckwith Close, Filbury Industrial Park, Leighton Buzzard for the following maintenance:

2 VDU screens for Model P2450
1 roller for printer PP156
Service overhaul for Model P2450

Invoice No 50521 for spares
   "   "   50522 for service

31

Word Processing Exercise 25

Learning Point Creating a document
Keying in text from manuscript
Producing a letter, memorandum and envelope
Printing documents

Ref TWB/ef

Mr D Robinson
Manager
Sec Secretarial Services

(use address given)

Dear Mr Robinson

We are in receipt of your order for repair and service to your machines. We feel one visit will be necessary and would be obliged if you could ensure the room and machines are available when our engineer calls at 10.00 AM Friday 23rd.

You will be invoiced as follows:

(Typist use invoice nos given)

MEMO ....
FROM   D Robinson (Manager)
To   Sally Thornton (WP Supervisor)

MAINTENANCE

Please ensure the WP room is available for a maintenance visit by the Service Engineer. He will need access from 10-3.00pm on Friday 23rd.

Word Processing   Exercise 26

Learning Point   Creating a document
Proof reading using correction signs
Keying in correct text
Printing documents

Before You Start   You will need a copy of the text below to complete this exercise. Either copy the text as it is and print out a copy or ask your tutor for a copy.

Task 1   Proofread the following text carefully and correct using appropriate manuscript correction signs.

```
AMSTERDAM - ''Venice of the North''

Experience the vibrant atmosphere of Amsterdamm. It is a
cosmopoliton city which combines both old-world charm and culture
with a modern eficient and exciting challenge. Its culture and
architectural beauty has earned it the reputation of being the
'Venice of the North.' There are museums, theaters and concert
halls including the world-famous Rijksmusem Museum and the Van
Goch museum.

Emsterdam bursts into life after dark with entertainment to
please all tastes. You can take in a concert, go to the theatre
or a nightclub, eat out or simply just stroll along the canal.
Amsterdam's liberal attitude to the infamous 'red light' district
is well kinown.

There are endles opportunities for a fascinating shopping spree
from flower markets, to shops offering crystal, diamonds,
silverware and cigars. If you wish to break for refreshment,
there are canalside cafes in abundance with delicious Dutch
specialities.

See Amstadam by cruising in one of the many glass topped boats,
relax and wattch the world go by. Amsterdam has something to
offer both young and old.
```

Task 2   Key in as much of the document as you can in 10 minutes, save under filename ... and print one copy.

If you typed the above exercise in 10 minutes with no more than two errors, you are ready to be assessed on NVQ Unit 3 Data Processing Elements 3.1 and 3.2.

Check your competence against the NVQ performance criteria on pages 48–9, then turn to the NVQ Practice Assignments on page 149.

The next word-processing exercises have been designed to develop your underpinning knowledge of word processing and increase your skills. They can be used for assessment of Unit 13 Element 13.3.

Word Processing Exercise 27

Learning Point Creating a document
Using indent facility
Printing a document

Task 1 Key in the following letter, setting 1" margins and leave 3" × 3" wide for a photograph as shown. Print one copy.

Before you start Many word processors have an indent facility to inset text from the left margin. Check your system notes.

THE CHESTNUTS RETIREMENT HOME — (centre)

3" × 3" for photograph

The superb appointed house provides a delightful residence for 30 people wishing to spend their retirement in a secure comfortable and caring home. Residents can enjoy a stimulating and independent life style within a safe and sympathetic environment.

NP [The care of our residents is of prime importance and is provided by our highly qualified resident SRN sister and SEN staff.

Care assistants are trained in-house and a visiting GP provides an adequate backup.

NP [Our home is managed by an experienced nursing officer.

The 24 rooms are divided into singles and doubles some with en-suite facilities. All rooms have hot and cold running water.

The following services are also provided:

Hairdressing   Flower Arranging   Bridge and whist evenings

Chiropody   Occupational Therapy

Physiotherapy   Visiting light entertainment Lectures and talks

Our kitchen staff are well-trained and experienced. Meals are served in the Dining Room except for special room service for occasions when residents may be poorly. /Cook *our resident* caters for all tastes and produces a tempting variety of meals.

The landscaped gardens are a unique feature with many rare and beautiful shrubs and trees.//Residents NP are free to wander and sit at will during warm weather.

Book Now!
and relax knowing
your future is secure

Enquiries to
~~Matron~~ The Nursing Officer

The Chestnuts

CRICKHOWELL

Powys

Tel 0241 682506
Fax 0241 675601

Word Processing   Exercise 28

Learning Point   Creating a document
Setting margins and tabs
Layout of notice of meeting
Printing a document
Photocopying

Task 1   Key in the following text as follows, and print one copy.

```
BLEASDALE SPORTS AND SOCIAL CLUB
Sports Centre
Bleasdale County Council
BLEASDALE
Lancs  BL12 L23

A meeting of the Committee of the Bleasdale Sports and
Social Club will be held in the Conference Room at the
Council offices on 12 April 1991.

AGENDA

1    Apologies
2    Minutes of the last meeting
3    Matters arising
4    Annual outing
5    Any other business
6    Date and time of next meeting


F GREENLAND
Secretary
```

Task 2   Produce sufficient copies of the Agenda to circulate to personnel invited to attend the meeting (see Exercise 29 which follows).

Word Processing   Exercise 29

Learning Point   Creating a document
Using indent facility (if applicable)
Layout of minutes
Printing a document
Checking paper supplied
Photocopying and distributing

Task 1   Key in the following text as follows, and print one copy.

```
MINUTES of a Committee Meeting of the Bleasdale Sports and
Social Club held in the Conference Room on 12 April 1991.

PRESENT

Mr R Gould
Mr D Blackham
Mrs J Gregory
Ms A Raybrook
Miss F Greenland (Secretary)

1   Apologies        Apologies were received from D Sasson
                     and G Timkins.

2   Minutes          The minutes of the last meeting were
                     read and signed as correct.

3   Matters arising  There were no matters arising.

4   Annual outing    It was unanimously agreed that the
                     annual outing should be to Ludlow Castle
                     for the Shakespearean performance.

5   AOB              There was no other business to discuss.

6   Next meeting     It was agreed that the next meeting be
                     held on 8 June 1991.


Chairman .....................

Date .....................
```

Task 2   Check printer paper supplies and print a copy. Reproduce seven more copies and distribute to all relevant personnel, keeping one for filing purposes. Ensure all copies are marked for specific personnel.

Word Processing   Exercise 30

Learning Point   Creating a document
Setting margins and tabs
Keying in text
Printing a document
Recalling a document
Moving text

Task 1   Key in the following with double spacing between numbered items, save under filename ... and print a copy.

Dear Client

SMALL BUSINESS INSURANCE

COMPASSURE has designed a specially-tailored insurance policy for small business systems. The insurance includes systems which consist of processors, input/output devices, screens, disks and printers.

WHAT DOES IT COVER?

3   Damage by flood

1   Loss or damage by fire or theft

2   Damage by failure of public electricity supply

WHAT DOES IT EXCLUDE?

3   Civil unrest, riot, strike, war

2   Normal wear and tear

1   The first £25 of any claim

Yours faithfully

DAVID ROSENBURG
General Manager

Task 2   Recall the exercise and change the numbers into their correct chronological order. Save and print the document.

Help Point   Check your system notes on how to move text.

Word Processing   Exercise 31

Learning Point   Creating a document
Setting margins and tabs
Keying in text
Printing a document
Recalling a document
Moving text

Task 1   Key in the following with double spacing between numbered items, save under filename … and print a copy.

```
JOB DESCRIPTION   Medical Secretary

EDUCATION         Good basic education including GCSE in
                  English and Mathematics

HOURS OF WORK     9-5.30 pm Monday to Friday

RATE OF PAY       £5900 per year

DUTIES AND RESPONSIBILITIES

1   Open incoming mail and process outgoing mail

6   Communicate with outside bodies, ie hospitals re
    outpatient appointments, tests and results and make
    transport bookings

3   Attend reception of patients at surgery times

2   Answer all incoming calls

5   Type all correspondence from Surgery

7   Communicate with Family Practitioner Committee

8   Order stationery including FPC forms as required

4   Extract patients' records during surgery
```

Task 2   Recall the exercise and move paragraphs into their correct chronological order. Save and print two copies of the document.

Word Processing   Exercise 32

SKILL BUILDING towards
NVQ Unit 13 Element 13.3

Learning Point Creating a document
Setting margins and tabs
Keying in text consistently
Printing a document
Recalling a document
Moving text

Task 1 Key in the following, without the corrections shown, save under filename ... and print one copy.

Task 2 Recall the exercise and correct as shown, print three copies, one for each doctor. Collate if necessary and distribute.

HIGHGROVE HEALTH CENTRE   *1" margins please*

Drs Shah, Gerrard and humley are all full-time practitioners and patients may make appointments to see any partner for a routine examination.

Appointments — *(caps & centre)*

All surgeries are by appointment only. Please telephone between 9.00 AM and 6.00 pm. URGENT cases will be seen at the earliest possible time. Please ring the surgery if you cannot keep an appointment.

SURGERY TIMES

MONDAY.	9 – 11.00 AM	4.00 – 6.00pm
TUESDAY	9 – 11.00	3.00 – 4.00
WED	9 – 11.00 AM	4.00 – 5.30
THURSDAY	9 – 11.00	2.00 – 4.00
FRIDAY	9 – 11.00	4.00 – 5.30

HOME VISITS

A Requests for home visits must be made by 10.00 AM. Please do not request a visit if it is possible for you to travel.

EMERGENCIES

Please telephone Highgrove 572601. If the surgery is open the doctor on duty will assist. Out of hours, a duty doctor is on call and your telephone will be interrupted with a message giving you the number to ring.

↘ A

40

DISPENSARY ARRANGEMENTS
*

We are allowed by the FPC to dispense to patients who live more than two miles from ~~the surgery~~ a chemist. For repeat prescriptions, hand into dispensary — allow 24hrs.

SUGGESTIONS

Any suggestions regarding our services to you should be made in writing to the Practice Manager.

NON URGENT CALLS

If you wish to discuss something with your ~~GP doctor~~ staf ring between 11.00 and 11.30 AM.

– – – New Page – – –

STAFF

Block centred on page

Sally Hanson	Practice Manager
Theresa Snow	Receptionist
Rita Meredith	Receptionist
Carla Snell	Secretary
Sonia Newman	District Nurse
Brenda Swallow	Midwife
Wendy O'Riordan	District Nurse
Dorothy Yates	Midwife
Lucretia Sharma	School Nurse

WELL ~~WOMAN~~ PERSON CLINIC
MONDAY   3 - 4.30

This clinic is run by our two district nurses who are available for consultations and advice

This paragraph before SUGGESTIONS

* Family Practitioner Committee

Be consistent throughout, 3 clear lines between sections please Typist

Help Point Block centring means centring the longest line and starting all text to be centred at that point.

Word Processing   Exercise 33

Learning Point   Consolidating previous skills
Setting margins and tabs
Indenting text
Printing a document
Photocopying

Task 1   Key in the following tours programme, and print one copy. Photocopy
three more copies for your folder.

EUROFUTUR TOURS
'THE DISCERNING TRAVELLER'

HOME AND OVERSEAS SUMMER/AUTUMN TOURS AND DAY TRIPS FOR 1992

31 May/3 June 1992	'Paris & Normandy – 3 days B/B including visit to Royal Palace of Versaille, evening cruise on Seine	£125.00
17 June 1992	'Cliff Richard and The Shadows' at Wembley Stadium, includes visit to Windsor Castle and buffet meal	£ 45.00
17 June 1992	London Day Tour and West End Show 'Me and My Girl' (best seats)	£ 23.00
23 June 1992	'Ladies Day Tour at Ascot' Hospitality Package, including entry to Silver Ring, strawberries and cream	£ 65.00
26/28 June 1992	'Normandy and Bayeux tapestry' overnight ferry crossing with cabin one night B/B hotel. Shopping at Hypermarket on return journey	£ 85.00
27 July 1992	The Royal Welsh Show – Bwlch Wells	£ 5.00
7 August 1992	Day tour to Sidmouth and reserved seat at International Folklore Festival	£ 15.00
28/30 October 1992	Bruges and Ghent – a memorable weekend in the beautiful Gothic cities of Belgium. Two days B/B in a first class hotel. Visit to lace-making school	£165.00
13 November 1992	Evening visit to Weston floodlight carnival including light refreshments	£ 12.00

Word Processing   Exercise 34   **SKILL BUILDING**

Learning Point   Consolidating previous skills
Form design.

Task 1   Key in the following form and save.

```
                    Euroexchange Employment Centre
                            UK Branch
                         2 Watling Street
                         London EC4 2NT

Position required *
Preferred Country *
Requested Salary *
Date of Application *
Name of Applicant
Address *

          *

          *

          *

Tel: *
Date of Birth *
Qualifications *
Years' experience *
All information on this form will be treated as
strictly private and confidential.
```

Word Processing   Exercise 35

Learning Point   Recalling a form
Form filling
Printing a form

Task 1   Recall the form you created in Exercise 34 and complete using the
following information.

4 September 199...

Tel 071 564 273

15 Kingsmark Square
London W1

Euro exchange Employment Centre

UK Branch
2 Watling Street
LONDON EC4 2NT

Dear Sirs

I am anxious to seek employment in France as a Personal
Secretary. I have spent my holidays there for the past five
years.

I have a Stage III qualification in both Typing and
Word Processing and a GCSE Grade C in French, and I
have worked for 8 years.

My date of birth is 2nd June 1964 and at present
I am Personal Secretary to an accountant in the city.
I can provide references if necessary.
Yours faithfully
    Tracey Asbourn.

Word Processing   Exercise 36

Learning Point   Consolidating previous skills
Calculating specific space

Task 1   Key in the following brochure information, and print one copy.

SPANISH VILLAS

Villa Type A

This luxury villa has 3 bedrooms, an open plan kitchen, bathroom and separate toilet. The dining and living areas are generous. Two bedrooms have twin beds and fitted wardrobes and the third bedroom is fitted with bunks. A bed settee in the living area can sleep two more persons.

leave 2½" x 2" for picture

Villa Type B

This villa has two bedrooms with a bathroom and separate toilet. It has an open plan design with a kitchen and generous living and dining area. Both bedrooms have twin beds and a bed settee in the living area can sleep two persons. This villa also has ample storage area.

leave 3" x 2½" for picture

Villa Type C

This is a luxury villa with two bedrooms. The first bedroom has a double bed with fitted wardrobes bedroom furniture. The second bedroom has twin beds and a fitted wardrobe. There is an ample lounge area with views over the bay

// The kitchen/diner is spacious with a fitted kitchen housing a split-level cooker, fridge, washing machine and drier. There are electricity plugs in all areas and a TV point in both lounge area and bedrooms.

leave 2½" x 3½" for picture

Check your competence against the performance criteria for NVQ Unit 13.3 on page 49. Then turn to the NVQ practice assignments on page 149.

CLAIT Word processing assessment criteria

Element of certification	Assessment objectives	Performance criteria
1.1 Enter text	1.1.1 Initialise word processing system	a) System is switched on b) Program is loaded
	1.1.2 Enter text	a) Text is entered with not more than three data entry errors
1.2 Edit text	1.2.1 Insert text	a) Text is inserted where specified
	1.2.2 Delete text	b) Text is deleted as specified
	1.2.3 Move text	a) Text is moved as specified
	1.2.4 Replace words	a) Words are replaced where specified
1.3 Change the appearance	1.3.1 Change margins	a) Left and right hand margins are changed as specified
	1.3.2 Alter line spacing	a) Line spacing is altered as specified
	1.3.3 Control justification	a) Text is justified as specified and unjustified format is used as specified
	1.3.4 Embolden text	a) Text is emboldened as specified
	1.3.5 Centre text	a) Text is centred as specified
1.4 Save and print text	1.4.1 Save text	a) At least one text file is saved
	1.4.2 Print document	a) At least one document is printed
	1.4.3 Exit from system with data secure	a) Data is stored on disc b) Program is closed down

NVQ assessment criteria

NVQ UNIT 3   Data processing

Element 3.1   **Produce alphanumerical information in typewritten form**

Assessment guideline

Produce approximately 150 words or numeric equivalents in a ten-minute period with no more than two uncorrected or typographical errors.

PERFORMANCE CRITERIA – ACTIVITY

Use an alphanumeric QWERTY keyboard

Produce letter(s) or memoranda with envelopes within a 10-minute period with no more than 2 errors

Make necessary corrections

Maintain security and confidentiality

Identify and report faults promptly

UNDERPINNING SKILLS AND KNOWLEDGE

Machine, safety, care and routine maintenance (including diagnosis of faults)

Operation and use of keyboard layout

Fingering techniques

Posture/seating

Interpreting oral and written instructions

Planning layout of work

Error correction technique

Use of dictionaries/reference books/glossaries

Saving information, as appropriate

Printing facilities, as appropriate

Element 3.2   **Identify and mark errors on scripted material, for correction**

Assessment guideline

Correctly identify all errors in transcription on a minimum of ten documents.

PERFORMANCE CRITERIA – ACTIVITY

Correctly identify all errors in transcription on business documentation on 10 different occasions

Handwritten material

Typescript drafts

Data/text is clearly marked for amendment

All numerical data is checked for accuracy and any errors or omissions identified

Layout conforms to specification

Uncertainty in text is reported and amended, as directed

UNDERPINNING SKILLS AND KNOWLEDGE

Correct spelling and punctuation

Use of dictionaries and other reference books

Effective use of a calculator

Techniques for checking (e.g. two readers, use of ruler)

Appropriate correction marks/erasing and correction methods

Styles and formats used by organisation

NVQ UNIT 13   Information processing

Element 13.3   Access and print hard copy reports, summaries and documents

Assessment guideline

Evidence supported by two examples of documents printed from any of the following: spreadsheet accounts, stock, catalogue or word-processed document.

PERFORMANCE CRITERIA – ACTIVITY

Information correctly assessed by document/record/field, as directed

All printed output conforms to specification

Documents are correctly collated and distributed as directed

Security and confidentiality of information is always maintained

Faults/failures are identified and reported promptly

Operating, safety and maintenance procedures are followed at all times

Accessing and closing down system

Loading printer, setting print specification and replenishing paper feed

UNDERPINNING SKILLS AND KNOWLEDGE

Interpreting oral and written instructions (including manuals)

Diagnosing print problems

Safe operation, care and maintenance of equipment

Retrieval process

Common print methods/mechanisms

This element should be assessed either in workplace or training centre, use extra word processed documents and stock control exercises as evidence.

DATABASES

What is a database?

A database is a name given to a collection of information stored in an organised way so that the information can be easily retrieved when required. Information can be stored both manually (on paper) or electronically (on computer). A telephone directory is an example of a manual database. There are now many commercially written programs to run databases on a computer.

In a typical office before computers were commonplace, information was kept in filing cabinets. This is still true today, but in order to store vast amounts of information, it makes sense to use the powerful storage and retrieval potential of electronic databases.

Electronic databases do precisely the same thing as manual databases except that they are far more efficient and capable of storing far more in much smaller spaces.

To help you understand the concept of electronic databases, think of the information stored as shown in the following diagram.

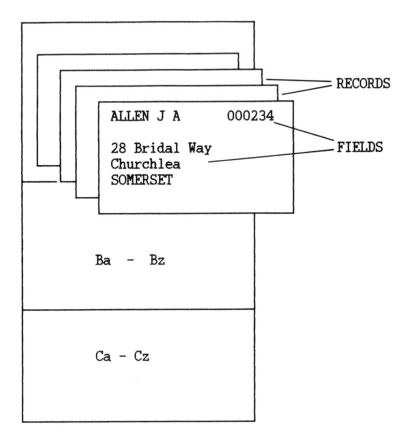

Figure 4   Comparing a manual and electronic database

Who uses databases?

Databases are used by any organisation needing to store large amounts of information, such as the Drivers Vehicle Licensing Centre Swansea, the DSS, the Police or a hospital. A typical database structure used in a hospital would be:

- FILENAME – Administration
- RECORDS – Patient
- FIELDS – contain Patients' details.

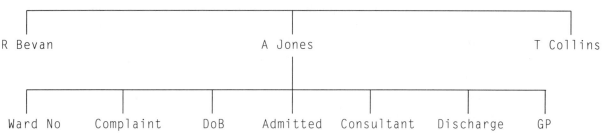

Figure 5 Possible structure of a hospital database

Although it is appreciated that the information has to be stored in a structured way, the information stored in FIELDS is known as DATA and is meaningless unless processed and output in a particular form. This is where the Database Management System or Electronic Filing Clerk comes into force in order to sort the data in specific order or to search and collate the data in a particular form.

What can a database management system do?

A database can only be useful if the information can be retrieved in a certain form. The Area Health Authority, for example, may need to use the database of a hospital to plan expense and organise the workforce. An Area Health Planning Committee may wish to know the following for statistical purposes:

- How many patients were admitted to a ward during a specific period.
- How many patients received a specific operation on the National Health.

Nuts and bolts of a database

Before you create a database you must give careful thought to what the database will be required to show. There are three stages involved in using databases:

- **Design:** deciding what data is to be held and how it is to be structured
- **Creation:** inputting the data structure
- **Management or interrogation:** searching for specific information or sorting the data into a specific form.

It is an important point to remember that the computer is a powerful tool which can rapidly sort enormous quantities of data, provided that it has been entered correctly. Similarly, to retrieve information, the computer has to be 'asked' the right questions, phrased correctly.

Designing a database

It is important to ask the following questions:

- How will the database be used?

- What type of data will be keyed in?
- How will the data be keyed in?
- What sort of enquiries will be made?

Database packages are designed in a number of ways and some require a specific FIELD TYPE to be entered. Others such as *Microsoft Works* allow input without specifying field types. For those systems requiring field types, some of the most common are:

- CHARACTER or ALPHANUMERIC – Fields used for text, a mixture of words, symbols and numbers, i.e. car registration numbers.
- NUMERIC – Fields used for numbers required for calculations.
- LOGIC – Fields suitable for data in which comparisons can be made, i.e. can the content of the field be True or False, Yes or No. One example is a field containing gender, i.e. M or F, Male/Female.
- DATE – Fields suitable for entering the date often appear in the following way: 00/00/00

Having made the necessary decisions regarding the purpose and size of the database, the database can then be created.

Creation of a database

Most database programs or packages are fairly USER FRIENDLY. The number of fields, name of field, type of field and width of field can be defined.

When NAMING a database file and fields, it is very important to use meaningful names which will simplify the enquiries made later. It is also important to use as little space as possible for the names because the data itself will take up a lot of computer memory. Early exercises in the database section give field names and field widths whilst later exercises give students the choice. System users requiring field types need to refer to this section.

Data protection

Details about everyone are entered on a computer somewhere from the time they are born. It is therefore very important that all this personal information is protected from unscrupulous people.

The Data Protection Act was introduced in order to protect people's rights. Anyone keeping a computerised database must now be registered and the individual has the right to see what personal information is being kept on record. The main principles of the Data Protection Act are that all information must be:

- fairly and lawfully collected and processed
- used for registered purposes
- accurate and up to date
- stored confidentially with appropriate security
- kept no longer than necessary for the registered purpose.

It is very important that an organisation's data is protected; some organisations go to great lengths to ensure this. Systems have passwords which enable only authorised personnel to access files. In spite of this computer hackers sometimes break password codes and great damage and expense can be caused by an unauthorised person gaining access to private computer files. Unscrupulous people have also introduced computer viruses to systems, wrecking data and costing vast sums of money and valuable time. When working for an organisation it is imperative to adhere to security procedures.

Database   Exercise 1

Learning Point   The concept of a database
Creating a manual database
Using records and fields to structure a database

Scenario   Make a database of everyone in the class to include their name, eye colour, hair colour and gender.

Task 1   Create a manual database by entering the following fields on a sheet of paper.

Before You Start   Take a sheet of A4 paper with the longest edge uppermost, and write in the following column headings:

SURNAME   FIRST NAME   EYE COLOUR   HAIR COLOUR   MALE/FEMALE

These headings are the FIELDS in which to store the students' details. Each student can be classed as a RECORD.

Task 2   Pass the sheet of paper to the next student to enter his/her details under the headings.

Task 3   Pass the sheet around the class until each sheet has the details of every student in the class. The completed sheets of paper form a manual database containing information about the class.

Task 4   List the contents of the sheets in ALPHABETICAL order and note the time taken to do so.

Remember   List information in alphabetical order of SURNAME starting from A to Z.

Database   Exercise 2

Learning Point   Creating an electronic database
Keying in data
Printing data

Scenario   Building a database of the class.

Task 1   Start up your system and create your database using the following specifications.

Before You Start   You are creating a database – check your system notes on how to do this. You are given the field name and field size. Check your system guide if your system requires more information.

```
FIELD NAME       WIDTH OF FIELD

SURNAME          20
FORENAME         20
EYECOL            5
HAIRCOL           6
GENDER            1 M(ale) or
                    F(emale)
```

Task 2   SAVE your database structure and enter your data using the class database.

Task 3   Check your entries are correct. When you are happy with the results, print one copy of all data.

Remember   Check your system notes on how to print a copy of your database.

Database   Exercise 3

Learning Point   Creating a database
Keying in data
Printing data

Scenario   You are secretary of your local Squash Club and have decided to put your club membership on computer. Design and create a database giving all members and their personal details. The club organises trips to folk festivals and members regularly pay in savings for this trip.

Task 1   Create your database using the following fields.

FIELD NAME	CHARACTERS WIDE	
SURNAME	11	
FORENAME	8	
ADDRESS1	21	
ADDRESS2	17	
POSTCODE	8	
DATE OF BIRTH (DOB)	8	
SAVINGS	2	0 decimal places

Before You Start   Follow your system guide on how to create and name your database file. You have been given field names and widths. These are only suggestions and it is important that you check through the data before creating the fields to check that each field will be large enough to take the longest details. Check your system guide if your system requires more information on field type.

If your system requests a number of decimal places for savings field, key in Ø.

Task 2   Once your database structure has been created, key in data as given below.

Help Point   Be consistent in entering data, i.e. use the same format for all entries. You will realise why when you come to search for data at a later stage.

PHILIPPA JONES
2 HIGH STREET
RICHMOND
RG1 2TN
02\03\69 £24

VERNON PATON
3 BRADFORD ROAD
RICHMOND
RG4 2TW
23\03\72 £15

JASON WILLIAMS
2 CRANFIELD DRIVE
CRANSTON
RG9 3NE
28\01\68 £15

DOMINIC WHITNEY
35 NEWTON AVENUE
BENSLEIGH
RG12 2WS
31\05\75 £5

STEPHEN ENDERSLEIGH
25 HIGH STREET
RICHMOND
RG1 2TN
04\05\75 £13

RICHARD BAKER
THE CHESTNUTS
BENSLEIGH
RG12 2WT
15\10\61 £15

TONY JACKSON
145 RICHMOND ROAD
CRANSTON
RG9 3NS
30\09\68 £15

SYLVIA STEPHENS
79 BRADFORD ROAD
RICHMOND
RG4 2TW
03\03\73 £24

TRACEY UNWIN
12 THE COPPINS
RICHMOND
RG2 7JT
02\06\72 £12

Task 3   Print a copy of the database with all your members listed in it.

Help Point   Check your notes on how to list details in your database.

Save this database for use later on.

Database Exercise 4

Learning Point Recalling a database
Editing records
Deleting a record
Printing

Scenario You are required to add new records and amend existing records on the Squash Club database.

Task 1 Recall the database you created in Exercise 3 and add the following records.

Before You Start Check your system guide on how to add on records.

```
GEORGINA STOCK         LINDA ERDSELY              KATHY HANCOCK
17 PITTVILLE AVENUE    34 RAVENSCRAG TERRACE      2 RIVERSIDE PARK
CRANSTON               BENSLEIGH                  FELIXTOWN
RG9 2NW                RG12 2ST                   FE1 R10
23\09\73 £12           07\02\78 £8                23\12\69 £15

RITCHIE COBURN         ROGER EDWARDS              LAWRENCE TIPPINGS
25 YEW TREE CLOSE      27 BRADFORD ROAD           THE MANSE
BENSLEIGH              RICHMOND                   BENSLEIGH
RG12 5ET               RG4 2TW                    RG12 2WN
17\07\75 £14           05\06\78 £2                29\11\69 £12

VERONICA SNELL         BENJAMIN COBB              PAUL STRIKER
10 LABURNUM AVENUE     10 TIP STREET              15 RIVERSIDE ROAD
BENSLEIGH              RICHMOND                   FELIXTOWN
RG12 2WT               RG1 4NW                    FE1 R11
04\04\74 £18           18\08\75 £7                23\03\77 £6
```

Task 2 Make corrections to your database records as given below.

```
Richard Baker's date of birth is 23\10\61 not 15\10\61.
Tony Jackson has £14 in the savings fund and not £15.
```

Task 3 Dominic Whitney has left the Squash Club and so his record should be deleted from the database.

Help Point Check your system guide.

Task 4 Print a complete list of your database. Save this database for use in a further exercise.

Database   Exercise 5

Learning Point   Recalling a database
Sorting records alphabetically (ascending)
Sorting on a numeric field (descending)
Printing

Scenario   Manage the Squash Club database.

Task 1   Recall the database you edited in Exercise 4 and check through to take note of the order of the records.

Task 2   SORT the database into ALPHABETICAL order of SURNAME (A–Z).

Help Point   In order to SORT a database you need to decide which FIELD you are going to SORT on. In this case it will be the NAME field. Check your system guide on how your particular system works.

You may also be asked whether or not to SORT in an ASCENDING or DESCENDING MANNER:

ASCENDING means A–Z or 1–100
DESCENDING means Z–A or 100–1

Task 3   Print a listing of the sorted database.

Task 4   Recall the database and SORT into DESCENDING order of amount of money paid into the savings fund.

Help Point   Choose SAVINGS field to sort on and choose DESCENDING order.

Task 5   Print a listing of the sorted database.

Database   Exercise 6

SKILL BUILDING towards
NEW CLAIT 2.1, 2.4
NVQ Unit 13 Element 13.1

Learning Point Creating a database
Selecting field width and type (if applicable)
Keying in data and printing
Saving

Scenario You are the owner of a garage and want to keep a record of all the cars you stock. Design and create a database to accommodate your stock of cars.

Task 1

Design and create a database to accommodate your stock as follows.

```
FIELD NAME

MAKE

MODEL

YEAR

ENGINE

STYLE

COLOUR
```

Before You Start You have been given FIELD NAMES but you will need to give the width of the fields. Check your data carefully for the longest entry.

Task 2

Key in the following data.

MAKE	MODEL	YEAR	ENGINE	STYLE	COLOUR
FORD	FIESTA	1984	1300	SALOON	RED
FORD	ESCORT	1987	1300	HATCH	GREEN
FORD	ORION	1986	1600	SALOON	BLUE
FORD	GRANADA	1989	1800	SALOON	GREY
FORD	GRANADA	1988	1800	SALOON	BLUE
VAUXHALL	CAVALIER	1984	1600	HATCH	GREEN
VAUXHALL	CAVALIER	1987	1600	SALOON	BROWN
VAUXHALL	NOVA	1989	1300	SALOON	RED
NISSAN	MICRA	1985	1300	SALOON	RED
NISSAN	MICRA	1987	1300	HATCH	GREY
NISSAN	MICRA	1984	1300	HATCH	BLUE
NISSAN	SUNNY	1983	1300	SALOON	BLUE
NISSAN	BLUEBIRD	1986	1500	SALOON	BLUE

Check your entries carefully.

Task 3

Print and save your database for use in a further exercise.

Database Exercise 7

Learning Point Recalling a database
Editing records
Adding new records
Deleting records
Printing and saving

Scenario Add and delete records on garage car stocks database.

Task 1 Recall the database you created in Exercise 6 and add the following records.

MAKE	MODEL	YEAR	ENGINE	STYLE	COLOUR
FORD	SIERRA	1986	1500	SALOON	WHITE
FORD	SIERRA	1984	1500	HATCH	BLACK
TOYOTA	COROLLA	1987	1300	SALOON	RED
TOYOTA	COROLLA	1989	1300	HATCH	RED
TOYOTA	CARINA	1988	1500	SALOON	GREY
TOYOTA	CELICA	1988	1500	SALOON	RED

Task 2 You have sold some of your cars; delete the records as follows:

VAUXHALL	CAVALIER	1984	1600	HATCH	GREEN
NISSAN	MICRA	1985	1300	SALOON	RED

Remember Follow your system guide as you did for your previous database exercise.

Task 3 You realise that you have made incorrect entries on some of your records. Check through your database and make the following corrections.

The 1984 Micra 1300 Hatch model is white and not blue and the Ford Fiesta saloon is grey not red.

Task 4 Print and save a copy of your database.

Task 5 Recall your database and SORT the database into ALPHABETICAL order of MODEL.

Remember You will need to specify which FIELD. In this case it will be the MODEL field. You will need to sort from A–Z. Check your system notes as you did for Exercise 5.

Task 6 Print a copy of the sorted database and save your file.

Two extra tasks follow for further practice if required.

Task 7 Recall your database and sort on vehicle age listing the oldest cars to the newest and print a copy.

Remember You will need to specify which field to sort on – in this case, it will be the YEAR field; use ASCENDING manner.

Task 8 Sort on COLOUR of vehicles, print a copy of the sorted database and save your file for further exercises.

Database   Exercise 8

Learning Point   Recalling a database
Searching for records meeting a specific condition
Printing and saving

Scenario   Using SEARCH facility on garage car stocks database.

Before You Start   Read the following notes to help you understand the SEARCH facility on databases before you attempt the tasks below.

It is possible to ask the Database Management System to SEARCH through the database until it finds a certain condition; for example asking the computer to SEARCH for all cars which are RED will result in a display of all cars for which the COLOUR FIELD has an entry of RED.

Remember   It is of particular importance that when you execute a SEARCH condition, you remember how the data was entered; for example the computer will not find 'red' if 'RED' was entered; it will not find 'Ford' if 'ford' was entered.

The computer needs to be asked the right questions. Different databases have different methods of 'phrasing questions' but certain principles do apply; for instance, to find out if a colour is red you must indicate that the search is on COLOUR field. Check your system guide for instructions on how to search your particular database.

Task 1   Recall the database you edited in Exercise 7 and check through the database to take note of how data was keyed in.

Task 2   Search through the database for all cars which are red and print a copy of the list.

Help Point   Your search should be on COLOUR field.

Task 3   Search through the database and print a list of all Ford cars.

Help Point   Search on MAKE field for every car listed as a Ford.

Task 4   Search through the database and print a list of all cars later than 1986 models.

Help Point   Your search should be on YEAR field. For example:

`>1986 means greater (later) than 1986`

Save your database for use in a further exercise.

Database   Exercise 9

Learning Point   Recalling a database
Searching to meet more than one condition
Sorting
Searching and printing the record
Deleting a record
Printing

Scenario   Search and delete records on garage car stocks database.

Task 1   Recall the database on garage car stocks you edited in Exercise 8 and execute a SEARCH through the records to establish how many cars registered in 1986 are blue in colour. Print out the list.

Before You Start   You will be searching the database on more than one criteria, i.e. meeting two conditions. First ask the database for YEAR = 1986 and combine with COLOUR = BLUE.

Task 2   Print out a complete list of all stock in DESCENDING order of year.

Help Point   This will require the SORT facility.

Task 3   SEARCH through and print out the record of the car you stock answering the following description, then DELETE the following record as having been sold.

FORD SIERRA 1986 engine c.c. 1500 WHITE SALOON

Help Point   This may be done in a variety of ways – check your system notes on how to do it.

Two optional tasks follow for further practice if required.

Task 4   Execute a SEARCH to establish how many TOYOTA cars are RED. Print and save your database.

Task 5   Execute a SEARCH to establish how many CAVALIER SALOONS you have in stock and print a list. You may delete your database file now if you wish after checking with your tutor.

Database   Exercise 10

Learning Point Design a database structure
Keying in data
Saving database
Recalling database
Adding records
Editing records
Printing

Scenario You are employed in the Personnel Department of a large retail chain in Manchester and have been asked to take responsibility for staff records. You are to computerise these (to save space you need not store addresses, as they are stored manually in personnel files). Suggestions for fields are:

```
SURNAME
FORENAME
SECTION
STARTDATE
TITLE
SALARY
TRAINING        Y(es) or N(o)
```

Before You Start You have been given FIELDS; you must study the data and decide the TYPE (if appropriate) and SIZE of the fields before creating the database.

Task 1 Create a database suitable to accommodate the staff details. Use a file name approved by your Centre.

Task 2 Enter the following details, taking care to enter data appropriately. Either choose the format below or use capitals as before.

```
Miss Joan Sempton 23 Victor Close Manchester MA1 8HT Ladies
Fashions started 23\05\85 Saleslady £10,500 trained

Ronald Horner 29 High Street Manchester MA1 2JT Menswear
started 23\06\83 Salesman £11,750 trained

Ms Sally Hansen 17 Laburnum Drive Manchester MA1 7JT China
started 30\09\89 Saleslady £10,000 non-trained

Timothy Whitehead 34 High Street Manchester MA1 2JT
Menswear started 15\02\89 Asst Salesman £8,500 non-trained

Rachel Habernash 98 Thames Road Manchester MA1 6JT China
started 17\05\89 Asst Saleslady £8,500 non-trained

Lawrence Highburn 12 Cherry Tree Close Manchester MA1 8JT
Hardware started 15\05\81 Supervisor £12,500 trained

Sebastian Johns 13 Maple Drive Manchester MA1 9JT started
19\12\84 Menswear Supervisor £12,500 trained

Mrs Janey Somers The Twigs Acacia Avenue Manchester MA1 5JT
China started 24\04\85 Supervisor £12,500 trained
```

```
Theresa Barclay 19 Devonshire Drive Manchester MA2 9BJ
Babywear started 29\02\85 Supervisor £12,500 trained
```

```
Sonya Simpson The Chestnuts Lime Grove Manchester MA1 4JT
ladies Fashions started 10\09\85 Snr Saleslady £13,000
trained
```

```
Linda Lucinton Haverley Pinewood Ridge Manchester MA2 1KT
Babywear started 07\07\89 Asst Saleslady £8,500 non-trained
```

Help Point   Check you have entered data correctly and consistently.

Task 3   Print a copy of all records in your database. Save your database.

Task 4   Recall your database and make the following corrections.

```
Sonya Simpson has left the firm and Joan Sempton has taken
her place with the subsequent change in title and salary
increased to £12,000.
```

```
Linda Lucinton and Rachel Habernash have both found other
employment and left the store.
```

Task 5   Add the records of the following staff who have been taken on.

```
Simon Phillips 412 Baker Street Manchester MA1 6HT Hardware
started 01\05\86 Salesman £9,000 non-trained
```

```
Bethan Williams Arosfa 23 Laburnum Drive Manchester MA1 7JT
Babywear started 08\10\87 Saleslady £9,000 trained
```

Task 6   Print one copy and save your database for use in a further exercise.

Database   Exercise 11

Learning Point   Recalling a database
Sorting
Searching
Printing out specified fields
Saving

Scenario   Using search and sort facilities on database of Personnel Department of a large retail chain in Manchester.

Before You Start   Read the notes given with Exercise 8 if you need to refresh your mind on understanding the SEARCH facility available on database systems.

Task 1   Management require a list of personnel in alphabetical order. SORT the database accordingly and print one copy.

Task 2   Employees of the company earning £10 000 and over per annum are entitled to a share bonus scheme. Print a list of employees to be given this opportunity.

Help Point   Search on SALARY FIELD for condition where salary=>£10 000.

Task 3   A list of supervisors is required for a forthcoming Board Meeting. Print out supervisors' NAME and DEPARTMENT only.

Help Point   Construct a field list and search on TITLE field for entries which equal Supervisor. Check your system on how to do this.

Task 4   Save your database for use in a further exercise.

Database Exercise 12

Learning Point Consolidating previous skills
Modifying database structure, i.e. adding a field
Printing one record only
Deleting a field
Sorting
Printing and saving

Scenario Modify database of Personnel Department of large retail chain in Manchester.

Task 1 The Personnel Department feels it needs information on staff leaving-dates. Since previous staff have had their records deleted, the information can only be recorded on staff leaving in the future.

Modify your database to include another field for this purpose.

Help Point Check your system notes on how to modify your database, i.e. change the structure.

Task 2 Sebastian Johns has handed in his notice to leave at the end of the month (use current month) as he has found alternative employment. Enter the information in his record.

Task 3 Print out the record for Sebastian Johns only.

Task 4 Management have decided that all employees taking up employment with the company will be 'in-house' trained and therefore do not need the TRAINING field information. Delete this field.

Help Point You will be changing the structure of your database; check your system notes.

Task 5 Save and print out your database in DESCENDING order of SALARY.

Database   Exercise 13

Learning Point   Consolidating previous skills
Designing and creating a database
Keying in data
Adding records
Adding a field
Sorting
Searching
Printing out specified fields only

Scenario   You work for a paper manufacturer and have been asked to put the stock on database for sales through their catalogue which they distribute through local stationers.

Task 1   Create a database using suitable fields and enter the following data.

CAT NO	DESCRIPTION	SIZE	COLOUR	WEIGHT (g)	PRICE (£)
9001	1 part woodfree	11"×9"	plain white	60	11.15
9002	1 part woodfree	11"×9"	music ruled	60	11.15
9003	1 part woodfree	11"×9.5"	plain white	60	11.25
9004	Letter quality	11"×8.5"	plain white	70	13.90
9005	2 part woodfree	11"×9.5"	plain white	54	21.95
9006	Letter quality	11"×8.25"	plain white	80	16.75
9007	Letter quality	11"×8.25"	plain white	90	19.95
9008	1 part woodfree	12"×8.25"	music ruled	70	15.45
9032	1 part woodfree	11"×14.5"	music ruled	60	14.95
9033	1 part mechanical	11"×14.5"	music ruled	70	15.95
9034	1 part recycled	11"×14.5"	music ruled	60	12.95
9036	2 part woodfree	11"×14.5"	music ruled	60	18.95

Task 2   Check your data has been entered correctly and print a copy of your database.

Task 3   Recall your database and add the following stock.

CAT NO	DESCRIPTION	SIZE	COLOUR	WEIGHT (g)	PRICE (£)
9040	1 part woodfree	11"×15"	music ruled	60	16.75
9041	2 part woodfree	11"×15"	music ruled	70	18.95
9042	1 part recycled	11"×15"	music ruled	60	14.95

Task 4   SORT your database into descending order of price and print your database.

Task 5   A customer wishes to know if there is any letter-quality paper in stock. List and print out all letter-quality paper.

Task 6

Add the following information.

Before You Start   Add another field called AMOUNT.

```
CAT NO
9001 9002 9003 9004 9005 9006 9007 9008 9032 9033 9034 9036

AMOUNT
2000 2000 2000 1000 1000 2000 2000 1000 500 500 1000 2000

CAT NO
9040 9041 9042

AMOUNT
500 500 1000
```

Task 7

Search for all paper with an amount of 500 and print catalogue number and paper type only.

Task 8

Print out your complete database.

Database   Exercise 14

Learning Point   Creating a database
Consolidating previous skills
Calculating on fields containing numbers

Scenario   You work for a tourist company offering accommodation in France. You are asked to key in the attached data which appears in their brochure.

Task 1   Create a database and key in the following data.

Before You Start   Make sure your cell widths will accommodate the data.

OWNER	LOCATION	AREA	SLEEPS	TAKEOVER	REF	COST
M Leclaircie	Belves	Dordogne	4	Saturday	DOR13	150
M Walbaum	La Baulle	Brittany	9	Saturday	BRIT10	300
T Collins	Les Eyzies	Dordogne	6	Saturday	DOR12	200
R Lomax	Saint-Coulitz	Brittany	9	Tuesday	BRIT02	280
M Le Foc	Plouescat	Brittany	4	Saturday	BRIT04	150
Mme Flanders	Orgnac-L'Aven	Ardeche	6	Saturday	ARD23	200
M Smith	Plouhinec	Brittany	5	Tuesday	BRIT12	175
M Le Brun	Le Guilvinec	Brittany	6	Tuesday	BRIT46	200
Ms Dauriac	Sarlat	Dordogne	8	Saturday	DOR28	250
Mme Pouchet	Saint-Genies	Dordogne	9	Tuesday	DOR98	295
M Le Ozille	Thueyts	Ardeche	4	Wednesday	ARD50	150
Mrs Yeates	Avignon	Ardeche	6	Saturday	ARD29	200

Task 2   Check your data has been entered correctly and print a copy of your database.

Task 3   SORT your database into alphabetical order of AREA.

Task 4   You have a client wishing to take a holiday in the Dordogne area. Search for and print details of suitable holidays for four people, with Saturday as the changeover day.

Task 5   SORT the holidays in order of lowest price to highest and print out details of the AREA and PRICE only.

Task 6   Print out a copy of your complete database.

The following tasks provide further practice if required.

Task 7   Calculate the total holiday cost.

Task 8   Calculate the average cost of the holiday.

Task 9   Calculate 2% company commission (if your system allows this).

Database   Exercise 15

**CONSOLIDATION EXERCISE
for NEW CLAIT 2.1, 2.2, 2.3, 2.4**

NVQ Unit 3 Element 3.3

Unit 13 Element 13.1

Learning Point   Creating a database
Consolidating previous skills

Scenario   You work for a garden centre which specialises in roses. The centre operates mail-order sales on a number of rose types and you have been asked to put the stock on database. Use a filename appropriate for your centre.

Task 1   Create a database using appropriate FIELD NAMES and enter the data below using the following codes.

Types	Floribunda rose	= FL	Fragrance	Slightly	= SF
	Shrub rose	= SH		Fragrant	= F
	Tea rose	= TE		Very	= VF
	Miniature rose	= MN			
	Rambler	= RA			
	Climber	= CL			

TYPE	ROSE	COLOUR	FRAGRANCE	ORDER NO	PRICE £
TE	Grandpa Dickson	Yellow	SF	TE01	
TE	Pascali	White	VF	TE02	
TE	Whiskey Mac	Orange	VF	TE03	
TE	Superstar	Pink	F	TE04	
TE	Silver Jubilee	Pink	SF	TE05	
FL	Allgold	Yellow	SF	FL01	
FL	Chinatown	Yellow	F	FL02	
FL	Elizabeth of Glamis	Pink	F	FL03	
FL	Iceberg	White	SF	FL04	
FL	Orange Sensation	Orange	F	FL05	
FL	Paddy McGready	Pink	SF	FL06	
MN	Angela Rippon	Orange	SF	MN01	
MN	Yellow Doll	Yellow	SF	MN02	
MN	Scarlet Gem	Red	SF	MN03	
MN	Pour Toi	White	SF	MN04	
MN	Little Flirt	Cerise	SF	MN05	
CL	Golden Showers	Yellow	F	CL01	
CL	Paul's Scarlet	Red	SF	CL02	
CL	Swan Lake	White	SF	CL03	
CL	Zepherine Drouhin	Pink	VF	CL04	
CL	Mermaid	Lemon	F	CL05	
RA	Albertine	Pink	VF	RA01	
RA	Emily Grey	Orange	F	RA02	
RA	Dorothy Perkins	Pink	F	RA03	
RA	New Dawn	Pink	F	RA04	
SH	Ballerina	Pink	SF	SH01	
SH	Canary Bird	Yellow	F	SH02	
SH	Frau Karl Druschki	White	F	SH03	
SH	Old Pink Moss	Pink	F	SH04	

Task 2   Check that all data is correct. Save and print a copy of your database.

Task 3   Recall your database and make the following corrections.

a) The following roses have become available and should be added to the stock:

- CL06 - Compassion, a very fragrant orange climbing rose
- CL07 - Pink Perpetue, a slightly fragrant pink climber.

b) The Superstar rose is not available at present, and needs to be deleted.

c) Pascali is a slightly fragrant rose and not very fragrant as entered.

Task 4   Sort the database into alphabetical order of TYPE and print a copy.

Database   Exercise 16

Learning Point   Consolidating previous skills
Modifying structure, i.e. adding a field
Calculation on field containing numbers

Scenario   Consolidate learned skills on the garden centre database.

Task 1   Recall the database you created in Exercise 15 and MODIFY your database to contain a new field for the price of each rose. Add the new details as given below.

ROSE	NO	PRICE £
Grandpa Dickson	TE01	2.50
Pascali	TE02	2.75
Whiskey Mac	TE03	2.50
Superstar	TE04	2.25
Silver Jubilee	TE05	2.75
Allgold	FL01	2.95
Chinatown	FL02	2.95
Elizabeth of Glamis	FL03	2.95
Iceberg	FL04	2.95
Orange Sensation	FL05	3.00
Paddy McGready	FL06	3.00
Angela Rippon	MN01	1.95
Yellow Doll	MN02	1.95
Scarlet Gem	MN03	1.75
Pour Toi	MN04	2.00
Little Flirt	MN05	1.75
Golden Showers	CL01	2.99
Paul's Scarlet	CL02	2.99
Swan Lake	CL03	3.25
Zepherine Drouhin	CL04	2.99
Mermaid	CL05	2.99
Compassion	CL06	2.99
Pink Perpetue	CL07	2.99
Albertine	RA01	2.99
Emily Grey	RA02	3.25
Dorothy Perkins	RA03	2.75
New Dawn	RA04	3.00
Ballerina	SH01	2.25
Canary Bird	SH02	2.25
Frau Karl Druschki	SH03	2.50
Old Pink Moss	SH04	2.25

Task 2   SORT database into alphabetical order of NAME.

Save and print a copy of the database.

Task 3   A customer wishes to order a very fragrant pink rose. Search the database and produce a list of the roses which fit this description.

Task 4   A customer has requested a list of all tea roses. Search the database and produce a list of all tea roses, printing out only ROSE and PRICE fields.

Task 5   SORT the database into order of PRICE in ascending order and print a copy.

Two optional tasks follow for further practice if required.

Task 6   SORT the database into alphabetical order of FRAGRANCE and print.

Task 7   SEARCH the database for all fragrant yellow roses and print.

Database   Exercise 17

Learning Point   Creating a database
Consolidating previous skills
Saving

Scenario   You are employed in a large firm manufacturing fitted kitchens and they are currently updating their brochure. You have been asked to put all stock offered in their brochure on a database to aid efficient access to sizes and price.

Task 1   Create a database and enter the following data.

Before You Start   Use your own FIELD NAMES, FIELD TYPE (if appropriate) and FIELD SIZE

UNIT	L/R HAND	CATALOGUE REF	COMPUTER CODE	PRICE
Wall Unit	Right hand	OW300	8864806	125.95
Wall Unit	Left hand	OW300	8864807	125.95
Wall Unit	Right hand	OW01	8864901	135.95
Wall Unit	Left hand	OW01	8864902	135.95
Wall Unit	Right hand	OW03	8864905	145.95
Wall Unit	Left hand	OW03	8864906	145.95
Wall Unit	Mobile	OW03	8864908	195.95
Floor Unit	Right hand	OF300	8664806	144.95
Floor Unit	Left hand	OF300	8664807	144.95
Floor Unit	Right hand	OF01	8664901	159.95
Floor Unit	Left hand	OF01	8664902	159.95
Floor Unit	Right hand	OF02	8664905	235.95
Floor Unit	Left hand	OF02	8664906	235.95
Floor Unit	Mobile	OF02	8664908	259.95
Drawerline	Right hand	DL300	8764806	159.95
Drawerline	Left hand	DL300	8764807	159.95
Drawerline	Right hand	DL01	8764801	162.95
Drawerline	Left hand	DL01	8764802	162.95
Drawerline	Right hand	DL02	8764815	169.95
Drawerline	Left hand	DL02	8764816	169.95
Drawerline	Mobile	DL03	8764818	239.95
Display	Right hand	DS300	8964806	259.95
Display	Left hand	DS300	8964807	259.95
Accessories	Utility	OP01	8564807	225.95
Accessories	Wine Rack	OP05	8564809	300.95
Accessories	Tray Unit	OP07	8564802	215.95
Accessories	Carousel	OP08	8564805	345.95

Task 2   Check you have entered the data correctly. Save and print your database.

Task 3   The price of units has risen recently. Amend your database accordingly.

- Display DS300 has increased in price to £265.95
- Utility OP01 has increased in price to £235.95
- The Carousel OP08 has been replaced with a new model OP09 8564806, at £350.00

Task 4   SORT your database into alphabetical order of unit. Save and print your database.

73

Database Exercise 18

Learning Point Recalling a database
Consolidating previous skills

Scenario Consolidate skills in searching, printing out specified fields only and modifying the database of a large firm of fitted kitchen manufacturers.

Task 1 You have forgotten to list the description of the units, i.e. the type of finish. Add a FIELD called DESCRIPTION to include the information.

- Units 300 are constructed in sapele.
- Units 01 are constructed in oak.
- Units 02 are constructed in pine.
- Units 03 are constructed in walnut.
- All accessories are in sapele.

Save and print your database.

Task 2 Recall your database to assist a customer who requires a list of all left-hand floor units.

Task 3 The local paper has rung asking for details of the firm's advertisement for the week. Produce a list of all walnut units, printing only UNIT, DESCRIPTION and PRICE.

Task 4 A customer requires a list of accessories: produce this list. You may delete your database after checking with your tutor.

Database   Exercise 19

Learning Point   Creating a database
Consolidating previous skills

Scenario   You are employed by a firm of book distributors in their
Purchasing Department. The following books have been
ordered from the publishers this month.

Task 1   Create a database and enter the books as follows.

Before You Start   Read the exercise through thoroughly, taking note of the
data to be entered. You will need to choose appropriate
FIELD NAMES, TYPES and SIZE. Enter data appropriately,
especially the author's name.

Roses, Jacqueline Seymour, Gardening, 5 ordered
The Face of Fear, Dean R. Koontz, Thriller, 50 ordered
Lightning, Dean R. Koontz, Thriller, 30 ordered
The Hunt for Red October, Tom Clancy, Thriller, 35 ordered
Diving Complete, George Rackham, Sport, 10 ordered
Synchronised Swimming, George Rackham, Sport, 10 ordered
The Science of Swimming, Mervyn Palmer, Sport, 10 ordered
Successful Propagation, Lucy Walton, Gardening, 65 ordered
Garden Planner, Avril Corkham, Gardening, 3 ordered
Plants of the British Isles, Barbara Nicholson, Gardening,
6 ordered
Come Pour the Wine, Cynthia Freeman, Romance, 12 ordered
Create Your Garden, Cecil Holder, Gardening, 2 ordered
Watchers, Dean R. Koontz, Thriller, 75 ordered
The Mask, Dean R. Koontz, Thriller, 100 ordered
Blott on the Landscape, Tom Sharpe, Comedy, 50 ordered
A Riotous Assembly, Tom Sharpe, Comedy, 25 ordered
Porterhouse Blue, Tom Sharpe, Comedy, 20 ordered
The Moon by Night, Pearl Buck, Romance, 25 ordered
The Golden Cup, Belva Plain, Romance, 20 ordered

Task 2   Check you have entered all data correctly. Print out a copy of the database.
Save your database.

Task 3   Recall your database and SORT into alphabetical order of book, type or
classification.

Task 4   Print your database and save.

Database Exercise 20

Learning Point Recalling a database
Consolidating previous skills

Scenario Consolidate skills in editing on the database of a firm of book distributors.

Task 1 Recall the document you created in Exercise 19 and make the following changes.

- Add a new Romance novel entitled *Evergreen* by Belva Plain; two customers have requested the book.
- 5 further books are required of *Roses* by J. Seymour.
- 30 copies of *Blott on the Landscape* are required instead of 50.

Task 2 Edit the FIELD containing Titles and increase the width to accommodate the new titles under the EDUCATION section.

Task 3 Add the following records.

Introducing Computers, Malcolm Peltu, Education, 100
Calculations for Commercial Students, Anne Campbell Education, 25
Beyond Word Processing, Peter Flewitt, Education, 50
Basic Clerical Procedures, Rita Martin, Education, 100
Basic Clerical Assignments, Rita Martin, Education, 100
Typewriting Dictionary, Pam Bennett, Education, 200

Task 4 Delete the following records.

The Moon by Night, Pearl Buck
Come Pour the Wine, Cynthia Freeman
The Hunt for Red October, Tom Clancy

Task 5 Add a new field to accommodate the publisher of each book.

Add the new publishers of each book as follows.

Title	Author	Publisher
The Golden Cup	Belva Plain	Fontana
Blott on the Landscape	Tom Sharpe	Penguin
A Riotous Assembly	Tom Sharpe	Penguin
Porterhouse Blue	Tom Sharpe	Penguin
The Face of Fear	Dean R. Koontz	Headline
Lightning	Dean R. Koontz	Headline
Watchers	Dean R. Koontz	Headline
The Mask	Dean R. Koontz	Headline
Diving Complete	George Rackham	Faber
Synchronised Swimming	George Rackham	Faber
The Science of Swimming	Mervyn Palmer	Pelham Books

Introducing Computers	Malcolm Peltu	NCC
Calculations for Commercial Students	Anne Campbell	Longman
Beyond Word Processing	Peter Flewitt	MacMillan
Basic Clerical Procedures	Rita Martin	Pitman
Basic Clerical Assignments	Rita Martin	Pitman
Typewriting Dictionary	Pam Bennett	Pitman
Roses	Jacqueline Seymour	Colour Library Int
Evergreen	Belva Plain	Fontana
Successful Propagation	Lucy Walton	Hodder & Stoughton
Garden Planner	Avril Corkham	Hodder & Stoughton
Create your garden	Cecil Holder	Hodder & Stoughton
Plants of the British Isles	Barbara Nicholson	Collins

Task 6   A customer requires a list of books by Dean R. Koontz; search and produce a list.

Task 7   Sort the database into alphabetical order of publisher.

Task 8   Print a copy of the whole database.

You have now covered all the skills required for the following assessments:

- RSA CLAIT – Database component.
- NVQ UNIT 3 Element 3.3 and UNIT 13 Element 13.1

Check your competence against the CLAIT and NVQ criteria, then turn to the practice assignments on page 164 for NVQ and page 178 for CLAIT.

CLAIT database assessment criteria

Element of certification	Assessment objectives	Performance criteria
2.1 Create a database structure and enter data	2.1.1 Initialise database system	a) System is switched on b) Program is loaded
	2.1.2 Create alpha-numeric and numeric fields	a) Fields are correctly specified including at least one which can be sorted alphabetically b) Fields are correctly specified including at least one which can be sorted numerically
	2.1.3 Enter data	a) All records are entered with at least one field encoded as specified b) Errors in no more than 3 data items
2.2 Edit data	2.2.1 Edit data	a) specified changes to more than one record made
	2.2.2 Add a record	a) One record is added to the file
	2.2.3 Delete a record	a) One record is deleted from the file
2.3 Manipulate data	2.3.1 Sort records alphabetically	a) Records are arranged in alphabetical order according to the content of a specified field
	2.3.2 Sort records numerically	a) Records are arranged in numerical order according to the contents of a specified field
	2.3.3 Select records specified by a single criterion	a) At least one record is selected according to a specified criterion
	2.3.4 Select records specified by more than one criterion	a) At least one record is selected according to at least two specified criteria
	2.3.5 Print specified fields from selected records	a) Data from specified fields are printed
2.4 Save a database and and print contents	2.4.1 Save data	a) Database structure and data are stored on disc
	2.4.2 Print data	a) All data items are printed on table format
	2.4.3 Exit from system with data secure	a) Data is stored on disc b) Program is closed down

NVQ assessment criteria

NVQ UNIT 3   Data processing

Element 3.3   **Update records in a computerised database**
Assessment guideline
Recall and update records in a computerised database inputting a minimum of 30 records on at least three separate occasions.

PERFORMANCE CRITERIA

The correct field is always accessed

Date is correctly transcribed and entered into appropriate fields

Security and confidentiality of information are always maintained

Faults/failures are promptly reported and symptoms accurately described

Operating and safety procedures are followed at all times

Detect and correct errors on screen

Search

Sort

Retrieve specified information

Save text/data

Copy text/date file to another disk/backup data file disk

UNDERPINNING SKILLS AND KNOWLEDGE

Reading and interpreting manufacturers' and/or organisations' instructions

Reading and interpreting variable quality manuscripts

Computer keyboarding and system of operation

Safe operation and care of equipment

Styles and formats of organisation including file naming conventions

Security and backup procedures

Formats for inputting data

Common system faults and symptoms

Planning and organising work within deadlines

NVQ UNIT 13.1   Information processing

Element 13.1   **Process records in a computerised database**
Assessment guideline
Create, recall and update records in a computerised database inputting a minimum of 30 records on at least three separate occasions on a minimum of two commercial database packages.

PERFORMANCE CRITERIA

Data file formats always conform to defined specifications

New data files are correctly created, amended and deleted as directed

Data is correctly transcribed and entered into identified fields

All database files are without transcription error

Backup files are always produced and stored safely

Requested information is located, accessed and retrieved within specified time constraints

Security and confidentiality of information is always maintained

Faults/failures are identified and reported promptly

Operating and safety procedures are followed at all times

UNDERPINNING KNOWLEDGE

Proofreading screen and printed documents

Security and backup procedures

Styles and formats of organisation including filenaming

Relevant aspects of Data Protection Act

SPREADSHEETS

What is a spreadsheet?

A spreadsheet is a worksheet for setting out calculations or tables of figures. A manual spreadsheet can be a large sheet of paper, ruled into columns and rows. Accountants or anyone dealing with finance would find a spreadsheet useful.

A computerised spreadsheet is a program/package for creating large electronic spreadsheets using the computer's memory. You can use it for any type of calculation you wish. All you need to do is to key in the correct figures and formulae, plus any headings (text) you wish and the computer does all the hard work for you.

Spreadsheets are divided into columns and rows identified by letters and numbers respectively. The squares formed by the intersecting rows and columns are called CELLS and must be identified by a CELL REFERENCE, for example A1 or H10. Any figure, formula or text must occupy a CELL of its own. Whichever CELL the cursor rests on is called the ACTIVE or CURRENT CELL. Electronic spreadsheets can have approximately 63 columns and 254 rows available.

What can a spreadsheet do?

The main advantages in preparing spreadsheets using a computer are:

- Calculations are performed quickly and accurately
- Figures may easily be altered with automatic recalculations
- Finished spreadsheet models/templates can be saved for reuse.

For example, spreadsheets can be prepared for:

- Budget layout
- Cash flow analysis
- Forecasting – forward planning of finance
- Presentation of financial information
- Presentation of graphical information.

Spreadsheet facilities can be enormously versatile and it only requires some imagination to use them to their full potential.

What does a spreadsheet look like?

There are many spreadsheets available, such as SuperCalc, Lotus 123, VPPLANNER and VuCALC. A typical spreadsheet layout is shown below.

Column letters   A cell

	A	B	C	D	E
1	A1				
2	JAN	FEB			
3					
4		12	12	+B4+C4	
5				D5	
6					

Row numbers

```
      A1 is CELL NUMBER (or ADDRESS)
Cell B2 contains the text ''FEB
Cell B4 contains the number 12
Cell D4 contains the FORMULA +B4+C4
```

Figure 6 A typical spreadsheet

Keying in data

Spreadsheets may require specific ways for data to be entered. Data may be identified as follows:

- TEXT   – not to be calculated
- NUMBERS – to be calculated
- FORMULA – to perform calculations by linking 2 or more cells.

TEXT must be entered preceded by either a single or a double quote, for example ''Stock or 'Stock, on some spreadsheets.

NUMBERS may be entered as normal, for example 15 or 20.

Some examples of FORMULA (or plural FORMULAE) are:

- `+A1+A2` `to add the contents of 2 cells`
- `+A1—A2` `to subtract`
- `+A1/A2` `to divide`
- `+A1*A2` `to multiply`

Remember You should note the division symbol / and the multiplication symbol *.

Some systems may use brackets to mean 'a formulae is following' while some spreadsheets require a plus sign +.

e.g. To multiply the contents of 2 cells `(A1*A2)` or `+A1*A2`

 Throughout this section, + will be used.

What is a range of cells?

A number of cells to be totalled can be called a RANGE.

To add up a number of cells a different type of FORMULA may be used for example to add A1 through to A10 type

```
sum(A1..A10)
```

or

```
@sum(A1:A10)
```

How to move around a spreadsheet

Movement around a spreadsheet is via the CURSOR. It is also possible to use a GOTO function key or HOME key.

Spreadsheet commands

Many spreadsheets have levels of command which usually appear at the top or bottom of the screen. Some spreadsheets use the / symbol to activate commands such as ERASE, COPY, SET RANGE while other systems use an ALT key. These levels of command can only become evident by experimenting with a spreadsheet.

Commands to SAVE, PRINT or ERASE spreadsheets can also be accessed through the COMMAND LINE illustrated below.

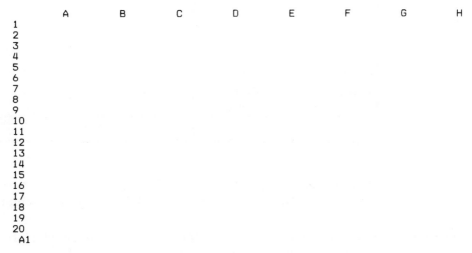

Figure 7   A spreadsheet command line

Spreadsheet Exercise 1

Learning Point Using a manual spreadsheet
Creating a spreadsheet on the computer
Entering text, numbers and formulae to multiply contents of
  two cells
Printing

Scenario You are the owner of a market stall selling second-hand books
and have decided to increase your income by selling small
items of stationery.

Task 1 Complete a manual spreadsheet using a calculator to show your total sales
for each item. Use the figures given below.

Before You Start Take a sheet of A4 paper and with the longest edge
uppermost, line up a spreadsheet as given in Figure 8.

Item	Cost Price	Sale Price	Number Sold	Total Sales
Ruler	0.35	0.95	24	
Pencil	0.18	0.36	52	
Rubber	0.24	0.45	34	
Pen	0.23	0.60	58	
Tippex	0.60	1.45	24	

EXAMPLE

	A	B	C	D	E	F	G
1	Item	Cost	Sale	Number	Total		
2		Price	Price	Sold	Sales		
3							
4	Ruler	0.35	0.95	24			
5							
6							
7							
8							

Figure 8

Help Point In order to calculate the total sales you will need to multiply the
SALE PRICE by the NUMBER SOLD, for example 0.95 × 24.

Task 2 When you have completed the manual spreadsheet, start up your system
and create a spreadsheet.

Help Point Follow your system guide to create your spreadsheet and enter
data. Do not enter totals.

Task 3 Use the appropriate formula to calculate the total sales for each item, print
and save your spreadsheet.

Help Point To calculate TOTAL SALES use the formula +C4*D4. Follow
system guides to print and save your spreadsheet.

Spreadsheet Exercise 2

Learning Point   Recalling a spreadsheet
Keying in additional data
Using formulae to a) Multiply the value of two cells
                           b) Subtract the value of two cells
Printing

Task 1   **Before You Start**   You will need to use two further columns – Total Cost and Profit.

Calculate the total cost of each item by using an appropriate formula.

Help Point   You will need to multiply the number sold by the cost price, i.e. +B4*D4.

	A	B	C	D	E	F	G
1	Item	Cost	Sale	Number	Total	Total	Profit
2		Price	Price	Sold	Sales	Cost	
3							
4	Ruler	0.35	0.95	24			
5							
6							
7							
8							
9							
10					Total	Profit	

Figure 9

Task 2   Calculate the profit on each item by subtracting the total cost from the total sales.

Help Point   Use the formulae +E4-F4.

Task 3   Print and save your spreadsheet.

Spreadsheet   Exercise 3

Learning Point   Creating a spreadsheet
Keying in data
Using formulae to calculate totals of rows and columns, i.e.
   totalling ranges
Printing

Scenario   The Hospital Dietician for whom you work has devised a low-fat menu for heart by-pass patients. You have been asked to calculate the daily and weekly cost per patient before the dietician's final recommendations to the Hospital Finance committee.

Costs for meals are as follows.

	BREAKFAST	LUNCH	DINNER	DAILY COST
Monday	0.75	1.85	2.65	
Tuesday	0.66	1.99	2.45	
Wednesday	0.82	1.66	2.79	
Thursday	0.70	2.15	3.12	
Friday	0.69	1.77	2.99	
Saturday	0.60	1.82	3.05	
Sunday	0.82	3.50	2.50	
WEEKLY				

Task 1   Complete the manual spreadsheet below to calculate the daily and weekly cost.

	BREAKFAST	LUNCH	DINNER	DAILY COST
Monday	0.75	1.85	2.65	
Tuesday				
Wednesday				
Thursday				
Friday				
Saturday				
Sunday				
WEEKLY				

Figure 10

Task 2   Key into a computerised spreadsheet using the appropriate formulae to calculate costs.

Help Point   You will need a different type of formula to total a range of cells. Some systems use formulae such as TOTAL(B4..B10) or SUM(B4:B10). Check your own system.

Spreadsheet   Exercise 4

Learning Point   Creating a spreadsheet
Keying in data
Using appropriate formulae to multiply contents of two cells
Using appropriate formulae to total rows and columns
Printing

Scenario   As a Stock Clerk in a mail order firm specialising in teenage clothes, you are asked to design and create a spreadsheet to illustrate stock values as follows.

Task 1   a)   Complete the data manually drawing up a spreadsheet following the layout shown in Figure 11.

```
Cat No        Item          Number    Cost      Sale
                                      Price     Price

YW 8453       Shirt          35        9.21     12.95
VH 9166       Jacket         46       20.35     39.99
BT 9197       Trousers       89       13.55     24.75
CF 9168       Trousers       12       12.67     23.50
ER 4741       Shellsuit      53       20.60     39.50
YW 8463       Shirt          16        9.00     12.65
ER 9171       Shellsuit      27       22.55     34.00
YC 9170       Shorts         31        5.50      9.99
YC 0998       Shorts        130        5.03      9.50
ER 9174       Shellsuit      85       23.59     45.00
GE 4221       Belt           78        1.35      5.99
GE 5260       Belt           45        0.98      3.99
```

b)   Start up your system and create a spreadsheet keying in the data you used manually except for calculated totals.

Help Point   Some systems require you to enter your text preceded by ".

Save and print your spreadsheet.

Task 2   Calculate the following:

a)   The total cost of each item.
b)   The total sale price of each item.

Help Point   You will need to use another two columns for the total cost and total sale price of each item.

Task 3   Calculate:

a)   The total cost value of entire stock.
b)   The total sale value of entire stock.

Help Point   Use appropriate formulae to total the columns.

87

Task 4 Save and print your spreadsheet.

Help Point Check your system notes on saving and printing.

Task 5 Recall and display your spreadsheet formulae, save and print.

Help Point It is possible to change the display format of cells so that the formulae used are displayed instead of the actual cell values. Check your system notes on how to do this.

	A	B	C	D	E	F	G
1							
2							
3							
4							
5							
6							
7							
8							
9							
10							
11							
12							
13							
14							
15							
16							
17							
18							
19							
20							

Figure 11 Teenage wear stock value spreadsheet

Spreadsheet Exercise 5

Learning Point Drawing up a manual spreadsheet
Creating a spreadsheet on computer
Using formulae to total columns
Linking cells or copying formulae
Saving and recalling a spreadsheet
Printing

Scenario Your boss feels it would be a good idea to use a spreadsheet to run the office petty cash system, using the spreadsheet facilities to restore the imprest each day.

Before You Start You are required to draw up manually and complete a petty cash sheet using the following headings:

VOUCHER	DATE	DETAILS
TOTAL	MISCELLANEOUS	TRAVEL
POSTAGE	STATIONERY	

Task 1 Drawing up a Petty Cash sheet, completing a record of the following for week beginning 13 July 1992.

On 13 July you are given a cash balance of £30. Enter this in the Receipts column and date the entry.

You are also given the following details. Enter in the appropriate columns using abbreviated headings to fit cell width.

Voucher	Date	Details	Total	Column headings
No 21	13/7/92	Flowers	2.30	Miscellaneous
No 22	14/7/92	Milk	3.45	Miscellaneous
No 23	15/7/92	Bus Fares	5.00	Travel
No 24	15/7/92	Cleaner	8.00	Miscellaneous
No 25	16/7/92	Stamps	5.80	Postage
No 26	17/7/92	Staples	1.89	Stationery

Task 2 Using your system, create a spreadsheet to record the petty cash sheet for week beginning 13 July 1992, heading the spreadsheet PETTY CASH.

Help Point Enter the date as text and not numbers. Use the entries from your manual spreadsheet, except the totals for which you will use the spreadsheet facilities.

Task 3 Use the appropriate formulae each time, total all columns. Check that the totals of the individual columns equal the sum of the total column.

Help Point You will need a formula to total columns.

Task 4 Using a suitable formula, calculate the balance and bring down in the usual way to restore the Imprest, i.e. restore the cash to the amount given in the float (£30).

Help Point To bring down the balance either use the COPY facility or LINK cell with + CELL NUMBER. Check your system notes if you are unsure on how to link or copy cells.

89

Task 5   Save and print your spreadsheet.

Task 6   Recall the spreadsheet and continue the following week's petty cash entries entering data in the appropriate columns:

Voucher	No 27	20/7/92	Polish	£1.65
	No 28	21/7/92	Taxi Fare	£1.45
	No 29	21/7/92	Envelopes	£0.85
	No 30	22/7/92	Soap	£0.75
	No 31	23/7/92	Stamps	£4.50
	No 32	23/7/92	Cleaner	£8.00
	No 33	24/7/92	Coffee	£1.75

Total all columns after checking figures are correct using an appropriate formula to total each column.

Task 7   Use COPY facility or LINK cell to bring down the balance and restore the Imprest using a suitable formula.

Help Point   Use the same method you used for Task 4.

Print your spreadsheet.

Task 8   What is the difference in the two weeks' expenditure? Use suitable formulae to calculate and enter the amount at the bottom of the sheet.

Display the formulae used and print the spreadsheet.

Help Point   Spreadsheets have a facility to display formulae used. Check your own system guide.

Spreadsheet Exercise 6

Learning Point Creating a spreadsheet
Keying in data
Linking cells
Multiplying and subtracting cell contents
Replicating cell contents relatively
Printing

Scenario You work for a gas supplier calculating a factory owner's heating bill. He has an agreement with you to pay on a yearly basis, although the costs are recorded monthly.

Task 1 Key in the following data as follows.

Before You Start Key in date preceded by a single quote ' unless your system automatically enters this. Link cells to repeat figures.

Date	Previous reading	Present reading	Number of litres used	Cost per litre
050390	294560	350023		
060490	350023	385490		
050590	385490	388365		
040690	388365	402345		
050790	402345	408978		
040890	408978	414990		
030990	414990	432000		
051090	432000	450030		
051190	450030	479900		
061290	479900	513455		
070191	513455	579867		
050291	579867	645645		

Help Point Calculate only the first month's readings by subtracting the present reading from the previous reading. Use another column heading, month. You may then REPLICATE the formula to do all the other months at one time. Check your system. It may just mean copying the cell with the formula in to the range of other cells. Note how the formulae in the other cells are relatively duplicated, i.e. each formula automatically has the correct row numbers.

Task 2 The cost per unit is the special industrial price of 0.18p and the monthly delivery charge is £15.80. Adding the necessary columns, calculate the total cost of usage for each month.

Help Point You will need to use two more columns – one for the delivery charge and one for the monthly bill.

Task 3 Calculate the yearly bill.

Help Point You will need to use an appropriate formula to calculate the total monthly column in order to reach the yearly figure.

Task 4 Save and print your spreadsheet.

91

Spreadsheet Exercise 7

Learning Point
Creating a spreadsheet
Keying in data
Increasing cell/column width
Inserting rows and columns
Subtracting
Saving and recalling
Printing

Scenario
You work for the Administration Section of a Local Authority and have been given the following revenue budgets to calculate in order to assess community charges.

Task 1
Key in the following figures.

Before You Start
Make sure your SERVICES column is wide enough to accommodate all text. Check your system notes on how to do this.

Blaenarfon Rural District Council:
Summary of Revenue Budget

	1990/1		1991/2	
	Expend	Income	Expend	Income
SERVICES				
Education	184309	26951	198761	27074
Social Services	37039	6492	35259	-
Highways	36686	10603	40576	27693
Police	38094	18515	43987	21656
Public Protection	9132	8734	10564	9898
Recreation	4576	4400	5764	5609
Tourism	4876	4765	4398	4287
Environmental Health	576	-	587	-
Refuse Collection	782	616	1287	845
Other Services	10613	9056	11967	10867
Contingency Provision	3805	3702	3967	3798

Task 2
On completion of keying in data, check your figures and enter the appropriate formulae to total first column. REPLICATE/DUPLICATE your formula to total all columns.

Save and print your spreadsheet.

Task 3
Recall your spreadsheet and insert a spare row after SERVICES and figures in order to display your spreadsheet more effectively.

Task 4
Add a further row after Tourism to display:

Housing Repairs	12008	11687	14967	12900

Task 5
Add a further column after each Income column to display deficit figures.

Help Point
The deficit figure for each year can be calculated by subtracting the Expenditure from the Income column.

Task 6
Calculate the total deficit for each year and print your spreadsheet.

Spreadsheet Exercise 8

Learning Point Creating a spreadsheet
Keying in data
Aligning contents of cells
Inserting rows and columns
Totalling columns
Saving, recalling and moving blocks/ranges of cells
Printing

Scenario You work for the Sales Division of an insurance company and have been asked to calculate policy sales figures for different branches.

Task 1 Design and create a spreadsheet to enter the following figures with year columns right-justified (aligned at the right).

```
POLICY VALUES IN £s
BRANCH              Year      Year      Year      Year
SALES               1987      1989      1986      1988

ALBURTON            260380    298670    299867    285987
FRINSBOROUGH        287654    299867    299987    277466
MORECOMBE           298567    298750    305869    280679
DEVENPORT           329678    358567    329568    297856
YARDALE             295687    295867    294578    295689
SWANTON             329678    329578    318267    289567
```

Task 2 Total each of the columns using a suitable range formula, print and save your spreadsheet. Use a formula to total columns.

Task 3 Recall your spreadsheet and display it more effectively by INSERTING two more ROWS after your heading. Add the following branches before SWANTON by INSERTING three more ROWS:

```
GRIMSBY             309678    295678    298567    305687
WOKINGTON           305678    329678    295687    285679
HAVANT              295687    305687    295786    285987
```

Task 4 **Before You Start** Most systems require that you MARK the block or range of cells in order to MOVE them.

Change the position of the columns so they appear in chronological order of year, i.e. 1986, 1987, 1988, 1989. Some systems require you to INSERT a COLUMN to accommodate the new block of cells to, otherwise the new block of cells will overwrite the existing cells. Check your system guide.

Task 5 Add another column to display 'increase in sales' and determine which branch obtained the greatest increase in sales between 1988 and 1989. Insert this information at the bottom of the spreadsheet.

Help Point You will need to subtract year 1988 from 1989. You can REPLICATE or DUPLICATE the formula to save time.

Print your spreadsheet.

Spreadsheet   Exercise 9

Learning Point Consolidating previous skills
Aligning contents of cells
Using formulae to multiply and total rows/columns
Deleting rows
Reading/recomputing totals if necessary
Displaying formulae
Printing

Scenario You work for your College Library and have been asked to design a spreadsheet to calculate costs of books on order.

Task 1 Design and create a spreadsheet to accommodate the following information, with titles left-justified and other columns right-justified.

```
BUSINESS STUDIES SECTION INVENTORY
WORD PROCESSING BOOKS
Title                                     Number   Price (£)  Value (£)

Information Processing                       6       5.95
Into Word Processing                         4       8.50
Practical Word Processing                    2      20.50
Word Processing Skills                       6       9.00
A Guide to Using Word Processors            12       5.95
The Electronic Office                        6      14.95
Word Processing for Beginners                6       9.95
Introducing Word Processing                 10      14.90
Easy Steps to Word Processing               25       4.75
Know your Word Processor                    10       7.95
Total
```

Task 2 Check that your figures are correct and insert a blank row after the main heading and again before the total, i.e. before and after to display the spreadsheet more effectively. Use a suitable formula to determine the value of each set of books.

Task 3 Use appropriate formulae to calculate total number of books, prices and overall value of books.

Task 4 Save and print your spreadsheet.

Task 5 Recall your spreadsheet and change book prices as follows:

```
                                                      £
Information Processing                       6       4.75
Word Processing Skills                       6      11.00
A Guide to Using Word Processors            12       7.95
Introducing Word Processing                 10      12.75
```

Help Point Some systems automatically readjust totals. Check your system guide.

Print your spreadsheet.

Task 6 Insert the new titles after *Word Processing for Beginners:*

		£
Word Processing with Ease	6	12.95
WP: What Does It Mean?	4	3.95
Using WPs	12	2.95

Task 7 Delete the row with the title *Information Processing* and also the row with *The Electronic Office.*

Remember   Check your system guide on how to DELETE ROWS.

Task 8 Adjust your values and totals.

Task 9 You have been told there is an overall increase of 2% on all book prices.

Use appropriate formulae to calculate these.

Insert a new value column and produce a listing of your spreadsheet (a) with values displayed and (b) with formulae displayed.

Spreadsheet   Exercise 10

Learning Point   Consolidating previous skills
Using formulae to multiply
Using percentages in calculations
Totalling rows
Displaying formulae
Printing

Scenario   You are the owner of a coach hire firm. Design and produce a spreadsheet to illustrate your range of trips, together with costs.

Task 1   Create a spreadsheet to show the following figures:

Before You Start   Increase the width of the column to accommodate town names.

Journey	Mileage	Mileage charge (£)	Mileage cost (£)	Hire charge (£)	Coach park (£)
Torquay	142				10.00
Weston	56				8.00
Teignmouth	95				9.00
Swansea	136				8.50
Minehead	103				7.50
Poole	143				8.50
Bournemouth	150				9.00
Brighton	175				10.00
Worthing	162				9.00
Hastings	195				10.00
Eastbourne	215				10.00
Southsea	230				9.00

Mileage charge:

● under 100 miles   £1.15 per mile
● 100 and over   £0.95p
● 150 and over   £0.75p.

Task 2   Calculate the mileage cost.

Help Point   To calculate mileage cost you will need to multiply mileage by mileage charge.

Task 3   Calculate the hire charge at 3% of mileage cost.

Help Point   Use the formula

`mileage cost * 3%, e.g.+D4*.03.`

Task 4   Calculate the cost of each journey.

Help Point   Add a TOTALS column to add the mileage cost, hire charge and coach park charge. Use appropriate formulae to total rows.

Task 5   Print and save your spreadsheet: a) values displayed
b) formulae displayed.

Spreadsheet   Exercise 11

Learning Point   Consolidating previous skills
Using percentages in calculations
Changing cell format to integers (rounded-up figures)
Changing cell format to two decimal places
Printing

Scenario   As a car dealer you need to calculate a breakdown of sales and cost figures on your sales. You allow a discount of 12% on the sale price of the car. The sale price is the car price plus car tax.

Task 1   Design and produce a spreadsheet to show the following figures, keying in text left-justified and formating cells to two decimal places.

Help Point   Check your system guide on changing the format of cells to display two decimal points.

Make of car	Car price (£)	Car tax (£)	Sale price (£)	Discount allowed (£)	Price discount (£)
Micra	3448.00	287.33			
Cherry	4294.00	357.83			
Sunny	4435.00	369.58			
Bluebird	5618.00	468.17			
Prairie	6620.00	521.67			
Silva	8826.00	735.50			
Laurel	8745.00	708.75			
Patrol	8505.00	708.75			
300ZX	13003.00	1083.58			

Task 2   Calculate the sale price. Sale price is car price plus car tax.

Task 3   Calculate the discount allowed.

Help Point   To calculate the discount allowed, you must calculate 12% of sale price, e.g. formula (Sale price *.12). Some systems accept a % key, i.e. (Sale price *12%).

Task 4   Calculate the Price less Discount.

Help Point   Use a formula (sale price − discount).

Save and print your spreadsheet.

Task 5   Recall your spreadsheet and calculate the VAT on each model at $17\frac{1}{2}$%.

Help Point   You will need to add another column for VAT. VAT is calculated at $17\frac{1}{2}$% on the sale price.

97

Task 6   Calculate the retail price on each car, which is discounted price plus VAT.

Help Point   Add another column for Retail Price.

Task 7   Recall your spreadsheet and change the cell format to display the figures in integer.

Help Point   Integers are rounded up figures, i.e. 15.85 would give an integer of 16. Check your system notes on how to change the whole of the spreadsheet to display integers. It is also well to note that you can set a particular range to integer if that is required.

Save and print your spreadsheet.

Two extra tasks follow for further practice if required.

Task 8   Change the cell format back to two decimal places. Calculate the dealer price whereby it is accepted that the dealer pays the original price before car tax is added, less 20%.

Help Point   You will need to add a column for Dealer's Price. Use a formula to calculate the dealer's price (Car Price minus 20% of car price), e.g. +B4−(B4*.20).

Task 9   Calculate the dealer's profit on the sale of all cars. Print your spreadsheet showing (a) values,   (b) formulae used.

Help Point   The dealer's profit would be the retail price minus dealer price.

Spreadsheet Exercise 12

Learning Point Recalling spreadsheet
Copying, erasing or blanking cells
Printing

Scenario You are the owner of an off-licence who places volume orders for spirits and wines. You have recently bought a computer and wish to keep an inventory on all your whisky purchases.

Task 1 Design and create a spreadsheet for the following data from January to December, right-justifying month headings and order number figures.

Before you start Some systems will not allow the months to be abbreviated. Check your system guide.

Brand	Order No.	Jan, Feb, etc.
Johnny Walker	0011131	
Grants	0011130	
Bells	0011125	
Glenfiddich	0011129	
Black & White	0011126	
Famous Grouse	0011128	
Pipers 100	0011133	
Royal Game	0011134	
Teachers	0011135	
Long John	0011132	

Task 2 Your supplier has written to say that he will supply ten cases per month of Grants, Bells, Teachers, Johnny Walker and five cases each of the other brands.

Remember You can use the COPY function on your spreadsheet to complete details for all months.

Task 3 Your supplier has now written to say that he will only supply eight cases of Bells per month because of a distributor's shortage.

Help Point Mark a range of cells and use the BLANK or ERASE facility to clear the months for Bells Whisky. Using the COPY range command, quickly insert eight cases.

Task 4 You have decided to stock Clandew and wish to include it on your inventory. Add this brand to the bottom of your spreadsheet with order number 0011127. Use the COPY range command to insert the same monthly amounts as for Glenfiddich whisky.

Remember You can use the COPY function on your spreadsheet to insert the same monthly amounts as Glenfiddich whisky.

Print your spreadsheet and save it for a further exercise.

Spreadsheet   Exercise 13

Learning Point   Recalling spreadsheet
Sorting data into specific order
Printing

Scenario   Recall the off-licence spreadsheet you created in Exercise 12.

Task 1   SORT the brands into alphabetical order.

Before You Start   Check your system notes on how to sort on a specific key or field. Don't forget to include all the spreadsheet; otherwise only the BRAND column will be sorted and the subsequent order numbers and amounts will stay as before. Systems may ask whether you want to sort in ASCENDING or DESCENDING manner. Choose ASCENDING.

ASCENDING means A–Z or 1–100.

Task 2   Print your spreadsheet.

Task 3   SORT the spreadsheet in descending order of Order Number.

Help Point   The key or field to sort on will be Order Number column and you will need to select DESCENDING manner.

DESCENDING means Z–A or 100–1.

Task 4   Print your spreadsheet.

Spreadsheet Exercise 14

Learning Point Consolidating previous skills
Cell protection
Deleting ranges
Printing

Scenario You work in the Wages Department of an organisation and have been asked to put the employees' PAYE records on a spreadsheet. Some activities are not included in CLAIT or NVQ assessments but are included as under-pinning skills.

Task 1 Key in the following data, locking cells to protect all headings.

Help Point Enter employee names and staff numbers as text. Ensure that the columns will accommodate data. Check your system guide on cell protection.

Employee	Staff No	No of hours Worked	Overtime Worked (hours)	Gross Pay (£)
Beddal J A	517043	40	4	
Young J	523042	30	-	
Price I	518210	40	-	
Chaplin J	521074	40	3	
Williams M	515672	40	2	
Johns M	521076	32	-	
Eldridge S	529678	40	4	
Kentish T	519856	40	2	

Note Normal hours are paid at £3.40 per hour; the rate for overtime is £4.50 per hour.

Task 2 Calculate the gross pay using new columns where necessary; format to two decimal places.

Task 3 Save and print your spreadsheet.

Task 4 Recall your spreadsheet and SORT into alphabetical order of names; print the spreadsheet.

Help Point Employee records should be sorted together with the names and not just the name column.

Four extra tasks follow for further practice if required.

Task 5 Add the following data.

Employee	NI (£)	Tax (£)	Net Pay (£)
Beddal	15.84		
Chaplin	12.65		
Eldridge	14.75		
Johns	15.84		
Kentish	10.76		
Price	10.76		
Williams	12.65		
Young	14.75		

Task 6   Calculate the tax on each employee at 30%.

Task 7   Calculate the net pay on each employee.

Help Point   Net pay is calculated by subtracting National Insurance and tax from gross pay. You will need to add another column for deductions. Make sure your column will accommodate the deductions.

Task 8   Unlock or take protect off then first set of headings and delete them. Print your spreadsheet showing both:

a)   actual cell values
b)   formulae used.

Spreadsheet Exercise 15

Learning Point Consolidating previous skills
Forecasting, using a 'What if' technique
Printing

Scenario You are the owner of a refreshment bar. In a normal day you serve people with a variety of snacks and drinks.

Task 1 Create a spreadsheet to illustrate your sales using the following data.

Before You Start You will need to increase the cell width in the goods column.

Goods	Number	Cost Price (£)	Total Cost (£)	Sale Price (£)	Total Sale (£)	Profit (£)
Tea	32	0.10		0.20		
Coffee	48	0.10		0.25		
Soft Drink	20	0.19		0.28		
Sandwiches	100	0.15		0.35		
Rolls	75	0.18		0.24		
Pasties	10	0.20		0.35		
Doughnuts	25	0.11		0.20		
Scones	27	0.13		0.23		
Fruit Cake	15	0.16		0.28		

Task 2 Use appropriate formulae to answer the following questions:

a) What is your total sale for the whole day?
b) What is your total cost outlay for the day?
c) What is your total sale of pasties?

Remember Use the appropriate formulae to calculate totals of rows and columns.

Task 3 Use appropriate formulae to answer the following:

a) What is your daily profit on sandwiches?
b) What is your total profit for the whole day?

Print a copy of your spreadsheet.

Task 4 **Before You Start** The WHAT IF technique is a method by which you alter a specific cell value to see what difference it makes to the rest of the spreadsheet. This can only be applied when cells are linked either by copying or duplicating cells.

a) Use the WHAT IF technique to calculate how many doughnuts you need to sell to increase your overall profit to £50 (nearest amount over £50).

Help Point Change the number of doughnuts sold and watch the profit total change until it reaches £50 or the nearest to £50.

b) How much must you charge for a cup of coffee to increase your coffee profit to over £10 (nearest to £10).

Help Point   Change the sale price of coffee and watch the totals change. Experiment until you find the nearest total to £10

Task 5   Print your spreadsheet showing:

a) cell values – with increased prices shown
b) formulae used.

Spreadsheet   Exercise 16

CONSOLIDATION EXERCISE for NEW CLAIT 3.1, 3.2, 3.3, 3.4

NVQ Unit 13 Element 13.2

Learning Point   Consolidating previous skills

Scenario   You work in the Accounts Department of a large supermarket chain with branches in South and West Wales. You are asked to use a spreadsheet to display sales figures for all branches.

Task 1   Key in the following spreadsheet headings and sales figures.

Before You Start   Widen your columns to accommodate the data. Format cells to commas to indicate the millions and thousands if the system allows.

Branches	1990-1	Groceries (£)	Household (£)	Kiosk (£)	Wines (£)
Pontypridd	1000000				
Cardiff	2800000				
Barry	1800000				
Swansea	2700000				
Cwmbran	1850000				
Caerleon	500000				
Caldicot	850000				
Ebbw Vale	1000000				
Pontypool	1500000				
Bridgend	1850000				
Newport	1950000				

Task 2   You are asked to calculate the actual sales figures for each department. You are given the percentage of the branch sales to work from as follows.

Branches	Groceries (%)	Household (%)	Kiosk (%)	Wines (%)
Pontypridd	66	9	15	10
Cardiff	70	8	13	9
Barry	65	7	14	14
Swansea	62	10	12	16
Cwmbran	75	8	12	5
Caerleon	71	5	14	10
Caldicot	89	1	6	4
Ebbw Vale	65	7	14	14
Pontypool	70	8	13	9
Bridgend	65	7	14	14
Newport	75	8	12	5

Help Point   Determine the actual amounts in £s using a formula to calculate the percentage of the branch overall sales. where possible replicate cells to avoid repetitive keying in.

Print a copy of your spreadsheet.

Task 3   The Caerleon branch has closed down and need not be included in the overall figures: delete the branch.

Task 4   Print your spreadsheet displaying the formula used and save your spreadsheet.

Task 5   Recall your spreadsheet and sort into alphabetical order of branches.

Task 6   A new store has been opened in Port Talbot and, as a new branch, has sales of £40 000. Grocery sales are 75% with non-food sales at 15% and kiosk and wine/spirit sales at 5% each. Insert this new branch in its correct alphabetical position in the spreadsheet.

Task 7   Total the sales for 1991 and print your spreadsheet.

You have now completed all the skills necessary for the following assessments:

- RSA CLAIT – Spreadsheet component.
- NVQ UNIT 13 Element 13.2

The next four exercises involve solving a business problem using a computer spreadsheet. These exercises will help develop your BTEC business skills.

Spreadsheet   Exercise 17

Learning Point   Using a spreadsheet to solve a business problem.

Scenario   As the owner of a small boutique you need to plan your finance strategy for the coming half-year.

Before You Start   It will be necessary to design an income and expenditure spreadsheet which will give you the flexibility of using a WHAT IF technique to plan your expenditure.

Task 1   Key in your information using the following spreadsheet outline as your basis.

	Jan	Feb	Mar	Apr	May	June
INCOME						
Sales (£)	9000.00	9680.75	9930.30	8682.45	9570.50	9670.25
EXPENDITURE						
Wages						
Rent						
Business tax						
Electricity						
Telephone						
Insurance						
New Stock						
Total Costs						
PROFIT						

Task 2   Enter the following data LINKING all cells.

Wages   - 2 part-time ladies earning £56 per week
Your salary - £1200 per month
Rent   - £664 per month
Business tax- £2000 per year paid in April and November
Electricity - £560 payable in January and £430 payable in March
Heating   - £175 per month
Telephone   - £250 payable in February and £305 payable in April
Insurance   - £500 payable on 5 April
Stock   - January   February   March   April   May   June
                    £6000   £4500   £7000   £5000   £5600   £7000

Task 3   Using appropriate formulae, calculate total costs and total sales to determine your profit made over 6 months.

Task 4   Print your spreadsheet displaying   a) values
                                                                      b) formulae used.   107

Task 5   a) Using a WHAT IF policy, determine by how much your January sales must have increased in order to achieve a profit of £1000 (or nearest).

Help Point   Adjust the value in the January sales column until the profit total reaches the nearest to £1000.

b) Your sales people have requested a substantial rise in wages. How much can you afford to pay them before your profit drops below £3000.

Help Point   Repeat the procedure as for (a) but adjust the sales people's wages until the profit total drops below £3000.

Task 6   Print your spreadsheet showing projected figures.

Spreadsheet Exercise 18

Learning Point Using a spreadsheet to solve a business problem.

Scenario You work in the Accounts Department of an organisation and have been asked to work on long-range sales planning. This involves projecting sales figures over a number of years.

Task 1 Key in the following sales and overhead figures, locking the cells containing headings.

	Last Year (£)	Current Year (£)	1993 (£)	1994 (£)
Actual sales	300 000	320 000	388 000	400 000
Sales cost	50	55	60	80
Transport cost	150	185	200	250
Gross profit				

Task 2 Calculate the gross profit in each year.

Help Point You may add another row if you feel it necessary.

Task 3 Print your spreadsheet showing formulae used and save your spreadsheet.

Task 4 Recall your spreadsheet. You have now been given the overheads figures, i.e. the expenditure of the organisation. Leave a few rows after gross profit and then key in the following figures.

	Last Year (£)	Current Year (£)	1993 (£)	1994 (£)
Wages	32 000	32 700	34 500	36 000
Other overheads	35 000	35 000	35 000	35 000

Task 5 You are required to calculate the net profit for each year.

Before You Start Add another row with the heading net profit. Net profit will be calculated by subtracting the overheads, i.e. wages and other, from the gross profit. Add any row headings you feel necessary.

Task 6 Print and save your spreadsheet showing both (a) values, (b) formulae used.

Task 7 Project new figures to include the following changes:

a) Negotiations with employee unions have resulted in salary increases to be paid out over two interim periods.
b) 6% to take effect in 1993 and a further 2.5% to take effect in 1994.
c) Actual sales increase by 10% in each year i.e. 1993 and 1994.

Help Point Delete the original wage figure for 1994.

Print a copy of your spreadsheet showing new values.

Spreadsheet Exercise 19

Learning Point Using a spreadsheet to solve a business problem.

Scenario Richard and Sarah are a newly-married couple who have recently purchased a three-bedroomed semi on a mortgage. Curtains and carpets were included in the sale and they have bought second-hand furniture with cash received as wedding presents. Richard will own his car once he has made a final payment of £85.57 for it in November but it has deteriorated over the past year and ideally he would like to change it. He uses it to travel to his work some 22 miles away and needs a reliable vehicle. Sarah works locally and earns £125.37 per week.

Richard works as a computer operator on £12 000 per annum less £173.35 per month deductions. He is familiar with spreadsheets and is very keen to sort out their financial standing over the next six months, starting in June, because they would like to buy a Hi-Fi system for Christmas.

Task 1 Design and create a spreadsheet using the following financial information. For estimation purposes, accept each month as having four weeks instead of being a calendar month.

```
Mortgage repayments per month £175.38
Insurances £2.50 per week
Heating per quarter (estimate) £82.87 due in July and
October
Electricity per quarter (estimate) £117.68 due in June and
September
Car insurance due August £90
Road tax due February £100
Petrol £20 per week
Food £42 per week
Clothes £100 per month
Pensions £100.24 per month
Private health insurance £8.95 per month each
Miscellaneous £10 per week
Savings £10 per week
Lunches £1.75 per day for Richard (5-day week)
Entertainment £12 per week
```

Help Point Enter applicable data only.

Task 2 Design the spreadsheet to illustrate the Income and Expenditure over six months. Richard refers to the difference between Income and Expenditure as the Slush Fund.

Total all income and expenditure for the six months and total all months. Print a copy of the spreadsheet with

a) values shown
b) formulae used.

Help Point Adjust column widths and format as necessary.

Task 3 Use spreadsheet facilities to answer the following.

a) Will Richard and Sarah have sufficient savings to buy a Hi-Fi system costing £300 in time for Christmas, not using December's wage and salary; if not, by how much do they need to increase their monthly savings?

b) Richard's lunches have increased to £2 a day. How much will this cost over six months?

Print a copy of the spreadsheet showing the new figures. Return to the original figures for the next task.

Task 4 Richard has forgotten that he has a bonus payment in August which amounts to 75% of his monthly salary. Richard can buy a newer car for £2750 plus the proceeds from his old model. Will he have sufficient in the Slush Fund? If not, by how much should they reduce their monthly entertainment spending in order to raise that sum?

Help Point To calculate this increased salary, use a formula to add up the salary for the month plus 75% of the salary for the month, i.e. `c1+(c1*.75)`. Take care that the bonus salary is included for August only. Use a What If approach to reduce entertainment spending.

Task 5 Richard prefers to work in rounded up figures. Change the cell values to display integers. Save and print the spreadsheet.

Scenario Steve has recently set up a road haulage business and needs to plan his finances over the next five years. He will need a spreadsheet illustrating his income and expenditure over the five years. He has managed, with a bank loan, to purchase a five-year-old six-wheeler lorry complete with a three-axle trailer, but the lorry will need replacing after five years and Steve would prefer at that time to buy a lorry outright with his profit. He will also have to take a wage out of the business during the five years, he proposes to take £250 per week.

Spreadsheet Exercise 20

Learning Point   Using a spreadsheet to solve a business problem.

Scenario   Steve has recently set up a road haulage business and needs to plan his finances over the next five years. He will need a spreadsheet illustrating his income and expenditure over the five years. He has managed, with a bank loan, to purchase a five-year-old six-wheeler lorry complete with a three-axle trailer, but the lorry will need replacing after five years and Steve would prefer at that time to buy a lorry outright with his profit. He will also have to take a wage out of the business during the five years, he proposes to take £250 per week.

Task 1   Design and create a spreadsheet illustrating Steve's finances, using the following figures.

```
Operator's Licence £160
Lorry - Bank loan over 5 years at £165 per month
Trailer - Bank loan over 3 years at £160 per month
Road tax £1200 a year
Full comprehensive insurance £109 monthly
Goods in transit insurance £17 per month
Average diesel £2000 per month
Maintenance check £50 per month
Oil change service £120 per month
Average parts cost £2500 per year
Average tyre cost £1800 per year
Average earnings per month £5000
```

Also take into account the amount he takes weekly out of the business.

Task 2   Will Steve have £50000 profit after five years in which to buy a new lorry outright?

Task 3   Save and print your spreadsheet.

Task 4 provides additional practice if required.

Task 4   Steve knows of another lorry for sale which would take £350 per month over three years to buy. He would like to expand his business by taking on another driver, paying him £300 per average week. How much profit can Steve expect to make in the first year, after the same running expenses are covered on the same earnings as himself?

CLAIT spreadsheet assessment criteria

Element of certification	Assessment objectives	Performance criteria
3.1 Create a spreadsheet	3.1.1 Initialise spreadsheet system	a) System is switched on b) Program is loaded
	3.1.2 Enter text	a) Text is entered with errors in no more than 3 cells
	3.1.3 Enter numeric data	a) Numeric data is entered with 100 per cent accuracy into cells corresponding to specified headings and labels
	3.1.4 Enter formulae	a) Formulae are entered which produce correct results b) Specified formulae are printed
3.2 Manipulate a spreadsheet	3.2.1 Edit spreadsheet data	a) Amendments are made to at least one specified cell b) At least one row/column is deleted
	3.2.2 Replicate entries	a) Formulae are replicated so that a formula generating values in one row/column is made to operate in the same way on equivalent values in at least one other specified row/column
	3.2.3 Extend spreadsheet	a) At least one row/column is inserted at a specified position
	3.2.4 Generate new values	a) Formulae are entered/replicated to produce values in the new row/column related to the existing data as specified
3.3 Use spreadsheet display features	3.3.1 Left and right justify text	a) Specified text items are displayed left justified b) Specified items are displayed right justified
	3.3.2 Change column width	a) The width of a specified column is changed
	3.3.3 Use integer and decimal formats	a) Specified numeric data are displayed in integer format b) Specified numeric data are displayed in decimal format to a specified accuracy
3.4 Save a spreadsheet and print its contents	3.4.1 Save spreadsheet	a) Spreadsheet is saved on disc
	3.4.2 Print spreadsheet display	a) Data is printed in rows and columns
	3.4.3 Exit from system with data secure	a) Data is stored on disc b) Program is closed down

NVQ assessment criteria

NVQ UNIT 13   Information processing

Element 13.2   **Process information in a spreadsheet**

Assessment guideline

Operate a spreadsheet package to create a spreadsheet, enter data and formulae to calculate and project on at least four separate occasions, using a commercial spreadsheet package with automatic options.

PERFORMANCE CRITERIA

Spreadsheet format always conforms to defined specification

Create new spreadsheet, save, delete entries

Spreadsheet correctly created, amended and deleted as directed

Data is correctly transcribed and entered into correctly identified files

Detect and correct errors on screen

All spreadsheets are without transcription error

Carry out automatic calculations

Search/sort relevant areas of spreadsheet

Backup files are always produced and stored safely – copy data file to another disk

Projections are correctly generated as directed

Security and confidentiality of information is always maintained

Faults/failures are identified and reported promptly

Operating and safety procedures are followed at all times

UNDERPINNING SKILLS AND KNOWLEDGE

Interpreting oral and written instructions

Business terminology

Planning and organising work within deadlines

Planning/matching desired formats with available software/hardware resources

Proofreading screen and print copy

Styles and format of organisation including file naming

Use of formulae

Safe operation, care and maintenance of equipment

Security and back-up procedures

FURTHER APPLICATIONS

Graphics

Words generated by a computer are known as text; pictures generated by computer are known as graphics. Graphics can be a pictorial illustration of data. A graphics/drawing package is a computer program which enables you to produce drawings and graphs.

What can a graphics facility produce?

Anyone wishing to illustrate numerical data can use a graphics facility. Some spreadsheets have a graphics facility inbuilt for the production of graphs or histograms; the data already present in the spreadsheet model can be used for plotting purposes.

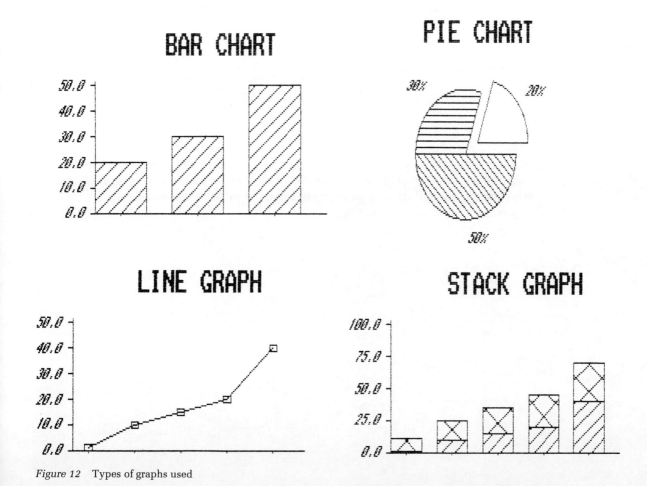

Figure 12   Types of graphs used

What can a drawing facility produce?

A drawing package can enable you to store the drawings, outlines and shapes you create to be retrieved later for editing. They can be retrieved at any time for use again and again, and can even be copied for illustration into other packages.

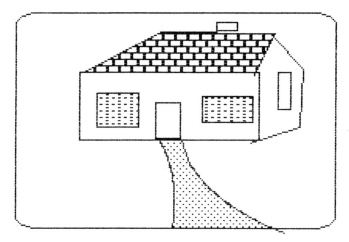

Figure 13   Drawing created on a graphics/drawing package

The shapes and symbols created can be filled with patterns to make more meaningful drawings; you can also enter text (labels). Computer capabilities of storing, retrieving and editing enable you to use designs for many different purposes.

Who uses these programs?

Anyone who wishes to promote the sale of their products would find this type of program useful. One of the most common users would be kitchen manufacturers who can design and fit custom-made kitchens to satisfy most people's requirements.

Graphics Exercise 1

Learning Point Plotting data for a bar chart, pie chart and line graph.

Scenario You work for a rainwear manufacturer who has asked you to illustrate sales of rainwear pictorially, i.e. in graph form.

Before You Start It is possible to select the graphics facility from your spreadsheet and enter the figures for each range separately for some graphs. Alternatively you could create a spreadsheet and use the cursor to indicate the data required for the graphics (this method is useful for bar or pie graphs in particular when ranges of text are needed).

Task 1 Use the following information to create a bar chart.

RAINWEAR SALES   January 500   February 300   March 200

a) Select the graphics facility and then the type of graph, e.g. BAR GRAPH in this instance.

Help Point To set the values for the bars, you will need to give a range value to illustrate them, i.e. A range = January sales, B = February sales, etc.

b) Set your data ranges (seek your tutor's help if necessary).

Help Point Some systems refer to the label of a bar as a legend. Select legend A and type in January, select B for February, etc. Most graphics programs have a viewing facility, so that you can check that you are entering data correctly.

c) Select a title for the graph and key in RAINCOAT SALES.

d) Set another title on the Y axis (the vertical axis of the graph) with the title No. of Raincoats. Print your graph.

Task 2 Clear your graph values and select a new graph type, a PIE CHART. Illustrate the following sales figures.

PERCENTAGE SALES

Raincoats 50%   Anoraks 30%   Rainhats 20%

a) Set the data ranges.

Help Point Two ranges are necessary to take the data, i.e. one range to take the words and another to take the values. Check your system on how to enter data.

b) Label each segment of your pie chart.

c) Give the graph the heading PERCENTAGE SALES and print the graph.

Task 3 Clear your graph values and select the type of graph for a LINE GRAPH.

a) Plot the three value points

January 500   February 300   March 200

b) Name the graph SALES TRENDS and print a copy of the graph.

Graphics   Exercise 2

Learning Point   Using a graphics package to:
Draw shapes/symbols
Label drawing
Edit drawing (delete shapes)
Print drawing

Scenario   You work for a manufacturer of bathroom suites who also installs them. You have been asked to use the computer to design a bathroom.

Task 1   Load your graphics/drawing package and produce the following outline.

Before You Start   Use the square tool to produce the items and the line-draw to produce the doorway.

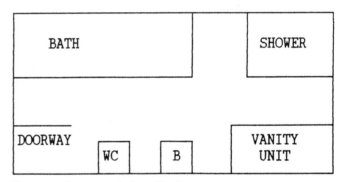

Figure 14   Computer-designed bathroom

Task 2   Label each item as in the illustration.

Task 3   The bathroom has a circular free-standing stool. Design the shape for a stool and store it.

Help Point   Use the circle-drawing tool for the stool.

Task 4   Position the stool in the drawing between the shower and vanity unit. Also copy and position the stool between the shower and the bath. Print your drawing.

Task 5   The buyers have decided they no longer need the vanity unit; erase it from your outline.

Task 6   Print your drawing.

Check your competence against the assessment criteria on page 120, and then turn to the CLAIT assignment on page 184.

Graphics   Exercise 3

Learning Point   Recall a drawing
Edit a shape
Fill a shape
Use patterns
Rotate an item
Add an item
Print drawing

Task 1   Recall the drawing you created in Exercise 2 and make the following changes.

Before You Start   Check your system is capable of the following tasks.

Task 2   Delete the stool positioned between the shower and bath.

Task 3   Draw a rectangular square for a linen basket and position between shower and bath, with the longest side facing the bath.

Task 4   Reduce the size of shower and print your drawing.

Task 5   Draw a square for a new vanity unit; edit with a circle inside for one wash basin.

Task 6   Rotate the linen basket so that the shortest side faces the bath.

Task 7   Fill the bath and shower unit with a pattern.

Task 8   Print your drawing.

CLAIT graphics assessment criteria

Element of certification	Assessment objectives	Performance criteria
4.1 Produce a defined	4.1.1 Initialise drawing system	a) System is switched on b) Program is loaded
	4.1.2 Draw shapes	a) Shapes are drawn as instructed
	4.1.3 Enter and position text	a) Text is entered and positioned as specified
4.2 Manipulate items	4.2.1 Copy an item	a) A specified item is copied and placed in another position
	4.2.2 Change size of an item	a) A specified item is increased and decreased in size
	4.2.3 Delete an item	a) An item is deleted.
	4.2.4 Edit a shape	a) A shape is adjusted as specified
4.3 Amend presentation	4.3.1 Fill shapes	a) Shapes are filled as specified
	4.3.2 Use patterns	a) Patterns are placed as specified.
	4.3.3 Rotate an item	a) A specified item is rotated as specified and placed in another position
4.4 Save and print an image	4.4.1 Save an image	a) An image is saved
	4.4.2 Print an image	a) An image is printed
	4.4.3 Exit from system with data secure	a) Data is stored on disc b) Program is closed down

Business/Accounting packages

Business/Accounting packages are computer programs used by organisations to process their data. Examples of these are payroll and accounting packages including stock control.

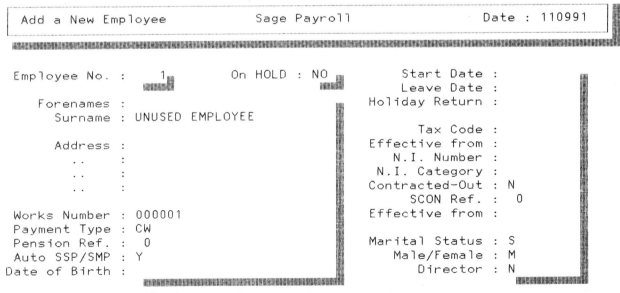

Figure 15 A typical payroll screen

Payroll

A computerised payroll package can take all the hard work out of the preparation of wages and salaries. A good program can calculate how much gross pay is owed to an employee from the number of hours worked, possibly entered via a clocking-on machine. PAYE (PAY-AS-YOU-EARN) is then calculated with National Insurance contributions and tax being deducted from an employee's gross pay. Calculations which would take a wages clerk hours to complete can be processed by a computerised payroll package in a fraction of the time.

Stock control

Figure 16   Don't be like Mother Hubbard and find your cupboard bare.

Most of us have bought an item out of stock at some time, whether from a shop or warehouse or spares section of a garage. Keeping a record of stock is of vital importance. No business wishes to store unrealistic levels of stock only to find popularity for that particular item has waned. Before the advent of computerised stock control programs, many organisations used stock cards to monitor the movement of stock and stock levels.

STATIONERY STOCK CARD						
Item					Max	
Unit Cost					Min	
Receipts			Issues			Balance
Date	Invoice	Qty	Date	Qty	Dept	Quantity

Figure 17   Manual stock control

Stock control packages run on computers are now used by most organisations. These packages monitor what is sold and calculate how many items are left, when stocks run low and when to re-order to maintain levels.

The CLAIT Scheme has a module for which either a payroll or stock control assignment can be completed. A stock control exercise has been included for practice; a stock control assignment has also been included in the CLAIT Assignment Section.

Stock control   Exercise 1

Learning Point   Using a stock control package to create stock records
Opening stock records
Setting up stock supplies
Editing records
Searching package
Issuing stock
Printing stock reports

Scenario   You work for a distributor of office supplies and have been asked to create the following stock records and maintain the computerised stock control system.

Before You Start   You will need to initialise or prepare your stock control program according to your system manual or tutor instructions. Data may not be listed as your system requires. Check with your tutor.

Task 1   Load your stock control program and create the following records, using only the data required by your own system.

Code	S001
Description	DRAWERLINE FLOOR UNIT L/H (S)
Unit Quantity	1
Re-order Level	30 (minimum level)
Re-order Quantity	70
Maximum level	100
Existing Balance	80
Cost Price	£75.00
Selling Price	£144.95

Code	S002
Description	DRAWERLINE FLOOR UNIT R/H (S)
Unit Quantity	1
Re-order Level	30 (minimum level)
Re-order Quantity	70
Maximum level	100
Existing Balance	65
Cost Price	£75.00
Selling Price	£144.95

Code	S003
Description	DRAWERLINE FLOOR UNIT L/H (D)
Unit Quantity	1
Re-order Level	30 (minimum level)
Re-order Quantity	70
Maximum level	100
Existing Balance	50
Cost Price	£45.00
Selling Price	£269.95

Code	S004
Description	DRAWERLINE FLOOR UNIT R/H (D)
Unit Quantity	1
Re-order Level	30 (minimum level)
Re-order Quantity	70
Maximum level	100

```
Existing Balance        45
Cost Price              £45.00
Selling Price           £269.95

Code                    S005
Description             WALL UNIT L/H (SINGLE)
Unit Quantity           1
Re-order Level          40 (minimum level)
Re-order Quantity       60
Maximum level           100
Existing Balance        75
Cost Price              £60.00
Selling Price           £82.95

Code                    S006
Description             WALL UNIT R/H (SINGLE)
Unit Quantity           1
Re-order Level          40 (minimum level)
Re-order Quantity       60
Maximum level           100
Existing Balance        40
Cost Price              £60.00
Selling Price           £82.95

Code                    S007
Description             DISPLAY WALL UNIT L/H (S)
Unit Quantity           1
Re-order Level          10 (minimum level)
Re-order Quantity       40
Maximum level           50
Existing Balance        30
Cost Price              £100
Selling Price           £134.95

Code                    S008
Description             DISPLAY WALL UNIT R/H (S)
Unit Quantity           1
Re-order Level          10 (minimum level)
Re-order Quantity       40
Maximum level           50
Existing Balance        10
Cost Price              £100
Selling Price           £134.95

Code                    S009
Description             FLOOR LARDER UNIT
Unit Quantity           1
Re-order Level          15 (minimum level)
Re-order Quantity       10
Maximum level           25
Existing Balance        20
Cost Price              £200
Selling Price           £404.05

Code                    S010
Description             OVEN HOUSING UNIT
Unit Quantity           1
Re-order Level          5 (minimum level)
Re-order Quantity       10
Maximum level           15
Existing Balance        12
Cost Price              £150.50
Selling Price           £309.95
```

```
Code                    S011
Description             FLOOR CORNER UNIT
Unit Quantity          1
Re-order Level         30 (minimum level)
Re-order Quantity      20
Maximum level          50
Existing Balance       45
Cost Price             £85
Selling Price          £199.95

Code                    S012
Description             WALL CORNER UNIT
Unit Quantity          1
Re-order Level         50 (minimum level)
Re-order Quantity      25
Maximum level          75
Existing Balance       70
Cost Price             £95
Selling Price          £194.95
```

Task 2   Check that the data is correct and print out stock details.

Help Point   Check your system guide or seek tutor help.

Task 3   Set up your opening stock supplies

Help Point   To set up your stock supplies and have some stock in balance, order the amounts stated as 'existing balance' for each item. Some systems require you to transfer stock into balance: check your system.

Task 4   Print out stock details, checking that the stock balances are correct.

Task 5   Amend your stock records as follows.

Code S001 – the drawerline units have increased in price, and now cost £146.50.

Code S010 has increased in popularity; you need to amend the re-order quantity to 45 and maximum level to 50.

Task 6   Sales have been made in the following stocks. Key in the details:

Help Point   Follow your system guides on how to issue stock.

```
Stock code S001 - 5 drawerline floor units
Stock code S003 - 20 left-hand single wall units
Stock code S005 - 25 display wall units (left-hand, single)
Stock code S011 - 20 floor corner units
Stock code S012 - 10 wall corner units
```

Task 7   Print out a history of stock movements and note how your stock has moved.

Help Point   Some systems require stock records to be updated: check your system.

Task 8   Take delivery of the following stock.

```
60 × single right-hand wall units (code S006)
40 × display right-hand single display wall units (code S008)
```

Task 9   a) Search for any stock shortages and print out a list.
          b) Re-order stock where necessary.

        Help Point   Some systems have a facility to print out re-order lists and some systems can re-order automatically. Check your system.

Task 10   Print out a valuation of all stock and close down your system.

        Check your competence against the assessment criteria before turning to the CLAIT section.

        This exercise can also be used for NVQ Unit 13, Element 13.3.

CLAIT stock control assessment criteria

Element of certification	Assessment objectives	Performance criteria
7.1 Record stock control transactions	7.1.1 Initialise stock system	a) System is switched on b) Program is loaded
	7.1.2 Load stock files	a) Access is gained to stock control records
	7.1.3 Enter details of incoming stock on files	a) Individual records are updated with 100 per cent numeric accuracy
	7.1.4 Enter details of stock on files	a) Individual records are updated with 100 per cent accuracy
7.2 Adjust stock control records	7.2.1 Edit records	a) Records are edited as specified
	7.2.2 Create stock record for additional item	a) One new record is created with all details correctly entered
	7.2.3 Delete stock record for withdrawn item	a) One record is correctly deleted for item withdrawn
7.3 Produce stock control reports	7.3.1 Produce re-order list	a) One list of items to be re-ordered is printed out
	7.3.2 Produce summary reports showing value of stock held	a) Summary reports showing value of stock are printed out
7.4 Save and print stock records	7.4.1 Save stock records	a) Stock records are saved
	7.4.2 Print stock list	a) Stock list is printed as specified
	7.4.3 Exit from system with data secure	a) Data is stored on disc b) Program is closed down

VIDEOTEX

Videotex is the name given to Information Services including TELETEXT and
VIEWDATA.

What can Videotex do?

VIDEOTEX can put thousands of pages of information at the disposal of users
who have access to either a computer or television screen. Two types of
information services which come under the label of VIDEOTEX are TELETEXT
and VIEWDATA. TELETEXT can only be received while VIEWDATA is
interactive: it can be received and controlled by the user.

TELETEXT   Teletext is the information service broadcast through normal
television signals to televisions which are fitted with teletext equipment. Anyone
can receive teletext by purchasing this type of television set (for a higher cost than
an ordinary TV set). A remote control device can operate these services to select
specific information screens or frames.

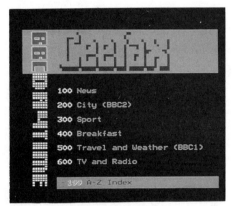

Figure 18   CEEFAX: the information service
broadcast by the BBC

Figure 19   ORACLE: the information service
broadcast by ITN

VIEWDATA   The best service of viewdata is PRESTEL, run by British Telecom.
Prestel can be received over a computer or private television screen by the use of
a MODEM and the renting of a British Telecom telephone line. Users have access
to the central Prestel computer. Other facilities such as electronic mail or
telebanking (moving money around) are available in addition to the information
service Prestel provides.

```
*88103
CitiService                        88103a        0p

NEWS time charge 31p/m            20-NOV-1991

 11 UK/World news      2 Brixton Break-Out
 12 Economic news        inquiry into role
 13 Market reports       of Special Branch
 14 Company news       3 CitiWatch
 15 Outlook              Dow expected to
 16 Prices               track higher
                       4 Soviet Woes
 17 Newsfile             Gorbachev details
    News from            economic decline
    18-Nov-1991

    ANALYSIS

 93 Junk food tops school dinners menu
 96 Waite became a name on his own list
 95 UK inflation falls to 3.7%

              0 YOUR MAIN INDEX
```

Figure 20   A Prestel frame

There are over 500 000 pages of information supplied by a variety of organisations or independent providers. Some local authorities have a viewdata system which can connect with the Times Network Service (TNS), a viewdata system for schools and colleges.

How is videotex organised?

A diagram below illustrates how screens of a videotex system are organised.

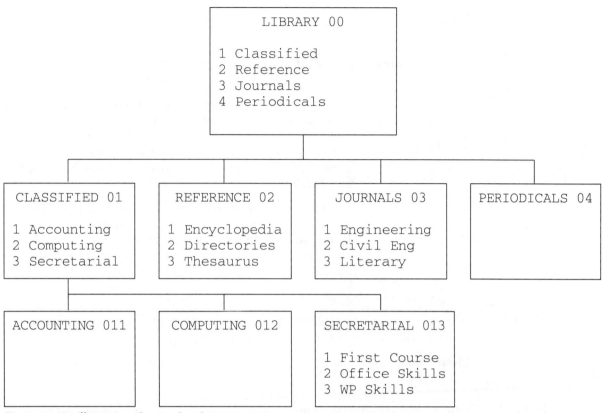

Figure 21   An illustration of a viewdata frame structure

A videotex system can store an enormous number of pages. It is important to note that these pages are indexed i.e. routed, so that pressing a particular number on an index page will result in another page being displayed:

Pressing the index number 1 on the opening page will call up page number 01.

Pressing the index number 3 on page 01 will call up page 013.

Electronic mail

It is not within the scope of this book to provide detailed information on ELECTRONIC MAIL or CONTROL TECHNOLOGY. These are included in the RSA CLAIT Syllabus, but as there are a number of electronic mail systems available you are advised to seek help from your tutors in learning how to use their system. Similarly with the Control Technology Module, you should consult your tutor and use the system manuals.

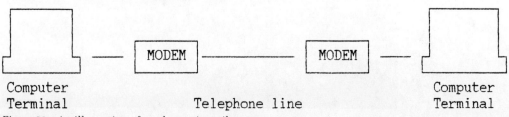

Figure 22   An illustration of an electronic mail system

Viewdata Exercise 1

Learning Point Logging onto a system
Accessing Prestel
Searching for information
Logging off system
Closing down

Scenario You work as an Assistant to a Public Relations Officer at
Supaware Computers Limited in Gloucester.

Periodically your boss organises conferences and seminars in
order to update customers with the company's latest products
and to give information about general trends in the computer
industry as seen from a manufacturer's point of view. Several
of the firm's customers are located in the North of England
and Scotland.

Your boss has asked you to assist in organising a suitable
location for the next conference and suggests a venue in
Birmingham or Bradford so that all parties can attend. He does
not mind whether the conference is housed at a hotel,
conference centre or university.

Task 1 Suggest a suitable location for the conference, giving the name and
address of the person to contact for booking purposes.

Help Point A suitable place to start would be on Prestel page 133050.

Task 2 The conference will commence on a Tuesday morning and end after
2.00 pm on Friday afternoon. Provide information on suitable trains for
personnel travelling from Gloucester and Manchester. The Gloucester
personnel do not want to travel earlier than 8.00 am on Tuesday.

Help Point Check British Rail timetables.

Task 3 One of the customers from Manchester is disabled, and although he will
be well looked after once he arrives at the Conference venue, he will need
some assistance while travelling. You need to establish what (if any) help
is available for disabled persons travelling alone.

Viewdata Exercise 2

Learning Point Logging onto a prepared viewdata file
Searching for information
Logging off system
closing down

Scenario The viewdata system is already in operation; see the
illustration on page 131.

Task 1 Log on to your viewdata system; go to page 2 and write down the name of
the principal town in Gwent.

Task 2 Trace the information on how many people live in Edinburgh.

Help Point Trace the page on Scotland. No more help now! You are on your
own.

Task 3 What is the population of Oxfordshire, England?

Task 4 What industries are there in Londonderry, Ireland?

Task 5 Return to the Main Menu and close down your system.

Viewdata   Exercise 3

Learning Point   Logging onto a prepared viewdata file
Searching for information
Editing a page
Creating a page
Printing a page
Closing down

Task 1   Log on to your viewdata system and find out what type of farming takes place on the South Coast in Hampshire.

Task 2   Go to page 2 and change the population of Newport, Gwent from 110 000 entered previously to 115 000.

Task 3   Go to page 0 and add:

```
5 Channel Islands
```

Task 4   Create a new page, number 5, and fill in the information as follows.

```
Page 5
                        ENGLAND
                  CHANNEL ISLANDS
                    1              2
Island           Jersey         Guernsey
Population        76000          45000
Principal Town    St Helier      St Peter Port
Population         50000          41000
```

*** Press 0 to return to the main menu.

Help Point   Check your system manual or seek tutor help.

Task 5   Test your viewdata system to ensure you have routed the page correctly.

Task 6   Return to the Main Menu and close down your system.

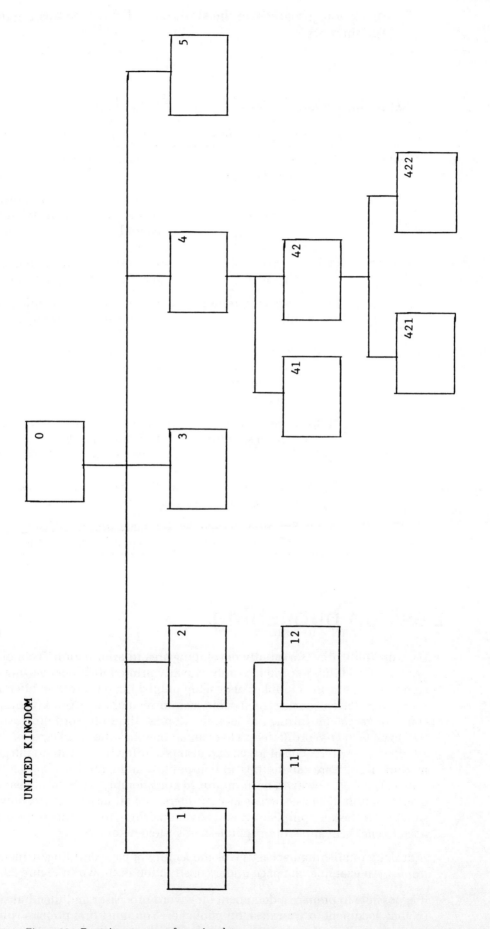

Figure 23   Routeing structure for a viewdata system

131

Check your progress on the skills checklist before turning to the CLAIT Assignments.

CLAIT Viewdata assessment criteria

Element of certification	Assessment objectives	Performance criteria
11.1 Set up a viewdata structure	11.1.1 Initialise viewdata system	a) System is switched on
	11.1.2 Create a directory	a) At least 10 pages are shown, prepared by the tutor and amended by the candidate to show routeing
11.2 Compose a viewdata page	11.2.1 Use special characters	a) At least two colours, one graphics and one flashing character are used
	11.2.2 Use background filling	a) Background area is filled with a contrasting colour or pattern
11.3 Route viewdata page	11.3.1 Route a complete page within a pre-determined structure	a) The page is shown on a menu and accessed accordingly
	11.3.2 Route pages using a structure	a) Tree structure is set up showing at least three levels b) Pages set up are all distinct
11.4 Save pages	11.4.1 Save newly created page	a) Newly created page is saved onto disc
	11.4.2 Exit from system with data secure	a) Data is stored on disc b) Program is closed down

Desktop publishing

Desktop Publishing is a rapidly developing area in Information Technology; it provides the ability to produce professionally printed documents using a desktop computer. There are a number of desktop publishing packages on offer, ranging from Aldus Pagemaker on the Apple Macintosh computer, Xerox Ventura on IBM compatible systems through to semi-desktop facilities on word processing packages such as WordPerfect. There are numerous other packages on the market all offering a wide range of fonts, and also providing the facility to integrate a mixture of software capabilities and output text and graphics to a professional finish. This has, however, been improved considerably with the advent of high quality output devices, such as laser printers. Not all laser printers, however, are suitable for desktop publishing, and anyone wishing to use this software would need to check manufacturers' guides and system manuals.

A desktop publishing package gives the facility of page building, using the term *frames.* An example of a page under construction is shown in Figure 24.

It is possible to prepare a document on a word processor and then transfer or 'call in' that document to your desktop publisher. You must first prepare your framework, i.e. decide on the page design. Desktop publisher packages normally

132

have inbuilt styles to choose from or you can design your own, as in Figure 25. By using a mouse to select icons you can achieve a highly professional finish. A typical desktop publisher screen is shown on the next page.

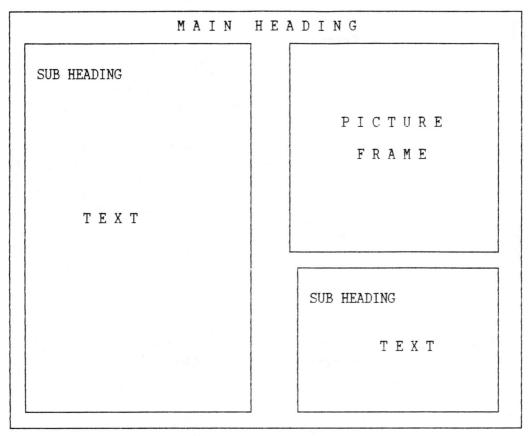

Figure 24   A typical desktop page frame

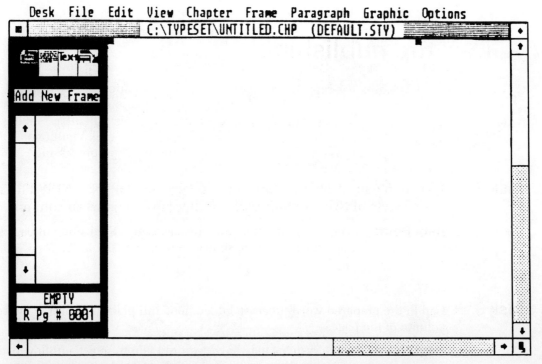

Figure 25   A desktop publisher control screen

Desktop publishing   Exercise 1

Learning Point   Preparing a document
Creating a desktop publishing file
Setting page format
Calling in prepared documents
Using styling functions
Printing

Scenario   You work for an Estate Agent offering properties in Spain.
You have been asked to use the exercise you created in
Word processing Exercise 36 on Spanish villas, and use it
to produce a brochure on the types of Spanish villas on
offer. At present only Villas Type A and B are available.

Before You Start   Locate the file you created for word processing Exercise 36,
delete Villa C information and re-adjust paragraphs so that
all text is left-justified; make a copy of this file for use with
the desktop publishing package.

Task 1   If you do not have the file, type in the following on your word processor,
save and make a back up copy for use with the desktop publishing
package.

SPANISH VILLAS

Villa Type A

This luxury villa has three bedrooms, an open-plan kitchen,
bathroom and separate toilet. The dining and living areas
are generous. Two bedrooms have twin beds and fitted
wardrobes and the third bedroom is fitted with bunks. A
bed-settee in the living area can sleep two more persons.

Villa Type B

This villa has two bedrooms with a bathroom and separate
toilet. It has an open-plan design with a kitchen and
generous living and dining area. Both bedrooms have twin
beds and a bed-settee and the living area can sleep two
persons. This villa also has ample storage area.

Task 2   Log on to your desktop publishing package and OPEN A NEW FILE; select
a page style of two columns with a gutter (space) between columns.

Help Point   Some desktop publishing packages give a selection of page styles.
You may use a book style or newspaper style.

Task 3   Call in the prepared word processed document and place it within the left-hand
column of the page.

Help Point   Some systems may have required you to select autoflow before
this. Consult your manual or ask your tutor for help.

Task 4   Once the document is in place, use the text editor to insert at least four lines between the main heading and subheading (Villa Type A). Similarly, insert at least ten lines after the end of the text, but before the next subheading (Villa Type B).

Task 5   Using the text styling functions, tag the main heading (SPANISH VILLAS) as a 'HEADLINE', and select a FONT with a print size of, say, 30 or the maximum your system will allow, if this is smaller.

Task 6   Still using the text styling functions, tag the subheadings (Villa Type A and Villa Type B) as 'Subheadings' and use another FONT with a print size of, say, 14.

Task 7   Print your document and save it with the filename VILLAS.

Desktop publishing   Exercise 2

Learning Point   Recalling a document
Creating boxes for pictures and text
Changing font type
Using text styling facilities
Editing frames
Printing

Task 1   Recall the document VILLAS you produced in Exercise 1. Using the text styling facility, centre the heading SPANISH VILLAS within the first column of the page. Change the font and print size to a different style and size of, say, 24. Select a serif font type.

Task 2   Draw a box around this heading, plus a smaller empty box in the second column for the firm's LOGO, to be put in later.

Task 3   Draw a picture/graphics box in the second column for each villa type as shown below.

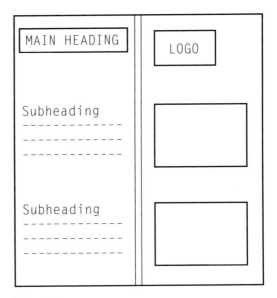

Figure 26

Task 4   Change the font and print size of the two subheadings to a different font and size of, say, 10 and if necessary adjust the position of the text and boxes so that the text is in the left-hand column opposite the areas where you have drawn the picture/graphic boxes in the right-hand column. (See above.)

Task 5   Using the text styling facilities, right-justify the text for both villa types.

Task 6   Using the frame editing facilities, cut and paste the subheadings, moving them to appear at or above the top-left-hand corner of each picture/ graphics box in the second column for the relevant type of villa.

Help Point   Check with your tutor to see if you need to create new frames to hold this text.

Task 7   Select a sans serif font type and print your document and resave the file. Your document should resemble the example shown below.

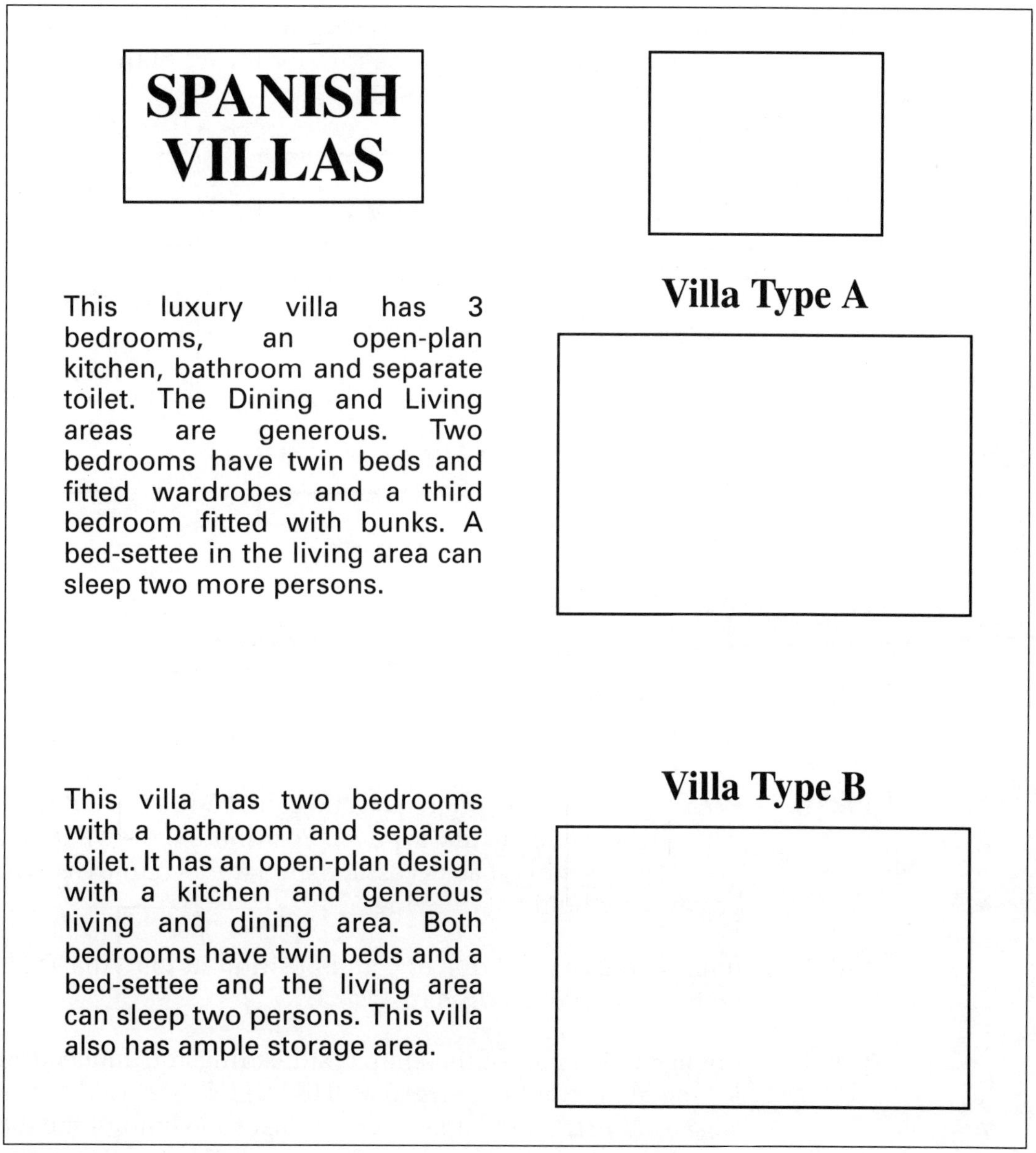

SPANISH VILLAS

Villa Type A

This luxury villa has 3 bedrooms, an open-plan kitchen, bathroom and separate toilet. The Dining and Living areas are generous. Two bedrooms have twin beds and fitted wardrobes and a third bedroom fitted with bunks. A bed-settee in the living area can sleep two more persons.

Villa Type B

This villa has two bedrooms with a bathroom and separate toilet. It has an open-plan design with a kitchen and generous living and dining area. Both bedrooms have twin beds and a bed-settee and the living area can sleep two persons. This villa also has ample storage area.

Figure 27

Desktop publishing   Exercise 3

Learning Point   Creating a document
Saving documents in different files
Recalling a document
Importing a document
Saving a document

Task 1   Using a drawing package or the drawing facility on your desktop publishing package, draw the interior layout of the two villas as follows.

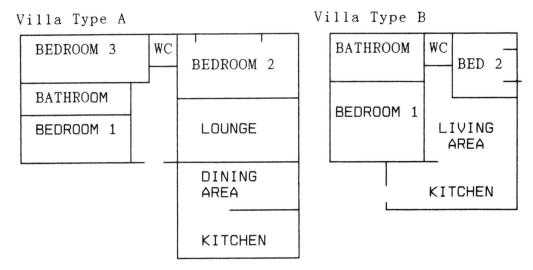

Villa Type A

Villa Type B

Figure 28

Task 2   Save your drawings in separate files.

Help Point   Seek a tutor's help for the next function.

Task 3   Recall your desktop published file called VILLAS and import (call in) your first drawing (Villa Type A). Position the drawing in the box provided, resizing it as necessary so that it occupies as much of the box as possible without overflowing.

Task 4   Import your second drawing and position in the Villa Type B graphics/picture box provided, as in Task 3.

Task 5   Change the values of the main text heading and subheadings as follows: for the main heading (tagged as 'HEADLINE') use a different font and a suggested print size larger than the last time but not the maximum possible. For the subheadings (tagged as 'Subheadings') use a different font and a suggested print size of 14.

Create a border to surround each of the columns separately and print your document.

Task 6   Save your file and close down your system.

You are now ready to tackle a basic CLAIT Assignment. Check your competence before turning to the CLAIT Assignment section on page 188.

CLAIT desktop publishing assessment criteria

Element of certification	Assessment objectives	Performance criteria
5.1 Set up page layout and import files	5.1.1 Initialise desktop publishing system	a) System is switched on b) Program is loaded
	5.1.2 Prepare page layout incorporating columns and a page wide heading	a) A4 page display is used b) There is space for a page wide heading and at least two columns
	5.1.3 Load prepared text	a) A previously prepared file is imported
	5.1.4 Load prepared image	a) At least one previously prepared image is imported
5.2 Display text effectively	5.2.1 Input text	a) At least 3 words are entered by means of the same keyboard
	5.2.2 Centre text	a) At least one heading is centred as specified
	5.2.3 Justify text	a) At least two paragraphs are justified as specified
	5.2.4 Use 3 type sizes	a) At least 3 different sizes of text are used as specified
	5.2.5 Use serif and sans serif	a) Serif and sans serif type faces are used
	5.2.6 Draw borders	a) Text and graphics are separated by lines/boxes
5.3 Change the presentation	5.3.1 Change size of text	a) Size of text is altered as specified to display an alternative layout fitting all the original material within the page
	5.3.2 Image is amended	a) The image is amended as specified in order to display an alternative layout fitting all the original material within the page
5.4 Save and print a document	5.4.1 Save document	a) A draft and the finished document are saved
	5.4.2 Print document	a) A draft and the finished document are printed
	5.4.3 Exit from system with data secure	a) Data is stored on disc b) Program is closed down

PART 2
ASSIGNMENTS

INTEGRATED ASSIGNMENTS

Integrated Assignment 1	**SKILL BUILDING towards** **BTEC PROBLEM-SOLVING** **BUSINESS SKILLS**

Learning Point Solving a business problem using IT
Using spreadsheet, word processing and database facilities, i.e. separate or integrated packages

Scenario You own a small family business, manufacturing ladies' clothing and have decided to purchase a personal computer to help you organise the business.

You are planning a new summer line in ladieswear and need to work out:

a) the cost of production to be in profit
b) how to create and maintain records of all garments
c) how to produce an advertisement.

SUMMER LINE DETAILS - garments made per week

40 Striped dresses - each dress requiring 3 metres of cotton @ £3.45 per metre.

60 Pleated cotton skirts - each skirt requiring 1.5 metres of polyester costing £2.95 per metre.

50 Short-sleeved tops - each top requiring 1 metre of stretch crepe at £3.50 per metre.

30 Cotton shorts - each requiring half a metre of cotton costing £3.25 per metre.

30 Trousers - each pair requiring 2.5 metres of acrylic @ £3.25 per metre.

20 Beach bags - each requiring a half metre of Egyptian cotton @ £2.50 per metre.

40 Head squares - each requiring a quarter of a metre of silk @ £3.50 per metre.

Add 25p per garment for extras, such as button, zips, thread, etc.

Add £3.00 each garment for labour.

Cost of new machine £350.

Task 1   Using a spreadsheet facility design a spreadsheet to illustrate the cost of making each item. Add a column for sale price, allowing a price which gives a 25% profit.

Use headings *metres, item, cost of material, labour, extras, total, sale price, profit.*

What is your overall profit? Illustrate with a printout of your spreadsheet.

Task 2   You wish to purchase a new machine. Have you sufficient profit?

Task 3   You have heard a rumour that labour costs will increase by approximately 5% over the next few months. How will this affect your overall profit? Print your spreadsheet showing projected figures.

Task 4   Design and create a database to store information of clothes manufactured, starting at a stock item number of 1000. Use fields to correspond with spreadsheet headings.

Task 5   Sort your database into ascending order of profit.

Task 6   Search your database and print out materials costing less than £3.00 a metre.

Task 7   You normally advertise your new lines in the Bestogs magazine. Design an advertisement on the word processor to cover your new stock.

Task 8   Key in a circular letter to your customers informing them of your prices; where possible, integrate part of your spreadsheet that gives item description and sale price. Your customers are:

- Sue Ellen's Boutique
- Lucy's Lot
- Wanda's Clothespeg.

Indicate on each letter the customer it is intended for and produce an extra copy for the file.

Integrated Assignment 2

Learning Point Solving a business problem using IT
Using spreadsheet, word processing and database facilities
either with integrated or separate packages

Scenario A relative has left you a farm on the Gower Peninsular, an area of outstanding beauty west of Swansea. Adjacent to the farm is a field housing 10 resident caravans (part of your relative's estate) which have been let to holiday-makers. You do not wish to continue with this arrangement but have decided instead to convert some of your farm buildings into holiday cottages and sell the caravans. You will need to construct a cash plan to consider the feasibility of the venture.

You have two barns which would be suitable for conversion to holiday accommodation for three families, with room for two adults and two children. Once the barn conversions are completed you are hoping to let the accommodation to families between Easter and October, which amounts to six months. The first three months will see only the weekends booked and there will be 13 weekends during that period. During summer months you will expect the accommodation to be booked throughout the week as well; this amounts to 12 weeks. Financial information is listed at the end of the exercise.

You have reached an amicable agreement with the families who have regularly stayed at the farm and have promised to give them priority booking on accommodation for the next three years. For easy reference, you have decided to keep a record of the families on a database. The families are listed in Task 3.

Task 1

Assuming that every booking is for an average family of two adults and two children, what will your financial position be during the first year?

Create a spreadsheet to illustrate your cash plan, in order to determine whether:

a) you will break even
b) run at a loss
c) be in profit.

Task 2

Print out a copy of your spreadsheet:

a) with values
b) with formulae.

Task 3

Create a database of caravan hirers and print one copy.

CARAVAN HOLIDAYMAKERS

Name	Address	Tel No	Caravan No	Month
Jones	23 Ferndale Swithin Nr Lincoln	568234	1	June
Elliot	Trident Watershot Yorkshire	342958	2	July
Richards	34 Turnball Close Didcot Reading	567978	3	June
Vester	23 Allen Drive Malpas Newport	633698	4	August
Cork	189 Cardiff Road Tonypandy Rhondda	234089	5	August
Stracher	2 Marina Walk Harefield Middlesex	569788	6	June
Royston	1 Hollywell Crescent Tring Herts	392845	7	July
Camberwell	34 Gabalfa Road Ely Cardiff	222756	8	June

Task 4

Run your database to list those families who prefer to holiday in June.

Task 5

Word process a letter to each family, integrating your database list of families if possible. Explain your plans and assure them that they have priority on bookings for the first three years.

Financial information

Barn Conversion Costs

You have been told that barn conversions are eligible for a 25% grant award:

Cost of barn conversions	£40000 for two
Community charge	£600/year
Lighting (estimate)	£750/year
Heating (average)	£500/year
Cleaner	£45/week for 24 weeks

Income

The sale of caravans has realised £15 000.

Accommodation

These charges will be as follows:

- Weekend charges are   Adult   £35
                          Child   £15
- Weekly charges are   Adult   £66
                        Child   £30

Integrated Assignment 3

Learning Point   Solving a business problem using IT
Using spreadsheet, word processing and database facilities
either as integrated or separate packages

Scenario   You are employed in the Accounts Department of the
Llanrhys Urban District Council and part of your duties is to
assist the Management Accountant.

The population of Llanrhys has grown rapidly since recent
industrial investment in the area, resulting in an increased
demand for more sports facilities. The Llanrhys Council has
therefore decided to add an extension of three squash courts
to the Llanrhys Leisure Complex.

The Leisure Complex is open seven days a week for fifty
weeks in the year and the car parking facilities are free. As the
only sports facility for a radius of twenty miles it has been
awarded a grant by Central Government towards the cost of
the extension. However, the present revenue of the complex is
unlikely to support this venture and a special meeting has
been held.

A number of proposals have been suggested at the meeting:

- A rise in subscription fees
- To levy a fee for car parking on all users of the complex,
  i.e. users not paying the yearly subscriptions
- To launch a more efficient method of fee collection, i.e.
  the set up and maintenance of a database of members

You have been asked to conduct a feasibility study, using a
spreadsheet, to ascertain whether the venture can be
supported, either on current income or by putting the
suggested proposals into effect.

Financial information

The initial cost of extension has been estimated at £¼ million.

- Maintenance costs   £50 000 pa   (rising by 5% each year)
- Heating   £4500 pa   (rising by 2% each year)
- Lighting   £2050 pa   (will be expected to
  have   10% rise in the fifth
  year)

To date there are 1000 members paying yearly subscriptions.

- Yearly subscription   £10
- Family tickets   £1.50 per day (per family of 4)
- Single tickets   50p per day (single users)

At the last survey it was estimated that 1800 users visited the Complex each
week, 1000 of which were single users. The remainder were in family groups.

The cost of the publicity drive would be £3500.

The government grant of £25 000 has been received.

Task 1   Design a spreadsheet showing expenditure and income expected over the five years commencing in 1991. *Note* Do not forget to link cells.

Task 2   Print your spreadsheet.

Task 3   Do the proposals of raising subscriptions or levying car parking fees need to be put into action? Amend the spreadsheet (using a WHAT IF approach) to show how the Complex can be in profit by the fifth year, either:

a) by raising subscriptions
b) by levying car parking fees.

Task 4   Print two copies of your spreadsheet to display:

a) values
b) formulae used.

Task 5   Construct a database of members on yearly subscription. Print out your database.

LIST OF MEMBERS

Name and Address	Sex	DOB	User Type	Fees 91	92
G Stone 23 High Street Loughor Dyfed	M	23/06/52	S	Y	Y
S Poulter 12 Broad Lane Penrhys W Glamorgan	F	12/07/64	S	Y	Y
J Stevens 13 Dillinger St Gorseinon W Glam	M	17/07/38	F	Y	Y
J Brown 12 Broad Lane Penrhys W Glamorgan	M	24/08/54	S	Y	Y
D King 30 Jakes Walk Landyssul W Glamorgan	F	23/10/34	F	N	N
C Norris 23 Green Lane, Penrhys W Glamorgan	M	15/03/38	F	Y	Y
J Hay Runnymead Poulters Lane Penrhys W Glam	M	24/11/65	S	N	Y
J Bollinger 145 King Street Road Penrhys	F	13/04/38	F	Y	Y
P Boulton Lli-ni 17 Station Road Llanmorlais	F	23/11/30	F	Y	Y
H Smith 12 The Walk Penclawdd W Glamorgan	M	02/06/42	F	Y	Y
A Walker 78 High Road Llanrhidian Nr Penrhys	F	14/09/71	S	Y	Y
R Sterry 58 Holly Road Penrhys W Glamorgan	F	23/04/69	S	Y	Y
E Wall 43 Bird Lane Penrhys West Glamorgan	F	12/01/67	F	Y	Y
B Groat 90 Main Street Gorseinon W Glamorgan	M	23/04/75	S	Y	Y
B Jarvis 23 Tide Row Llanmorlais Gower W Glam	M	15/05/33	F	N	Y
S Young 12 Station Road Llanmorlais Gower	M	17/03/63	F	N	N
A Tovey Step-a-side Loughor Road Penrhys	M	23/04/63	S	N	N
L Gerrard 12 Oystermouth Road, Mumbles W Glam	F	15/05/38	F	Y	Y

Task 6   Run the database and produce a list of members in alphabetical order.

Task 7   Run the database and produce a list of people in arrears of their subscription fees for year 1992, printing out only their name and address.

Task 8   Use the word processor to produce a circular letter to members stating the current fee (you can decide the amount that you think is necessary) for the year.

Task 9   Draft a memorandum to the Management Accountant making your recommendations and your reasons and integrate your spreadsheet if possible.

NVQ PRACTICE ASSIGNMENTS

Practice Assignment 1: Unit 3 – Element 3.1

Learning Point Producing alpha/numeric information in typewritten form in 10 minutes with no more than two errors.

Scenario You are employed as a secretary in the administration section of an independent training agency. You have been asked by Mr Harold Tenbury to word process two documents.

Task 1 Key in the following letter, together with an envelope.

```
Our Ref  HP/

12 August 1991

Training Manager
City Times Insurance Company
12 The Parade
SWINDON
Wilts
SW5 8TH

Dear Madam

Further to our telephone conversation, I would like to confirm the
arrangements for my students' visit to your premises on Thursday
afternoon of the 20 August. There will be 15 students and one
member of staff and I would like them to see the following
sections:

Reprographics
Computer Room
Data Preparation
Print Room.

Thank you for your kindness in arranging this visit at short
notice.

Yours faithfully
```

```
HAROLD TENBURY
LEARNRITE Training Agency
```

Task 2

Key in the following memo with today's date and send it to Jeremy Hawkins.

MEMORANDUM

From

To

Date

The study notes you require are not available at present;
however, I have asked Administration to prepare two more
copies of the set I received two days ago. I understand you
have been given the responsibility for resources. I have a
new course starting next month: could you supply the
following?

12   OHTs
12   A4 lined paper pads
12   Ringbinders with company logo

Practice Assignment 2: Unit 3 – Element 3.1

Learning Point Complete both Tasks 1 and 2 within a ten-minute period with no more than two errors.

Task 1 Key in the following letter with an envelope.

```
                    HOMESURE DOMESTIC INSURANCE COMPANY
                              23 Liversea Road
                                 Hammersley
                                 PORTSMOUTH
                                  PO2 5TM

Today's date

Mrs T Howell
34 The Yews
Havant
Portsmouth
PO4 3KV

Dear Mrs Howell

I have much pleasure in enclosing your Domestic Insurance
policy and extending a welcome to our Company. Our Domestic
Insurance is proving very popular with people wishing to
safeguard their home appliances and customers can feel
confident in the knowledge that they can rely on us.

Please keep your policy in a safe place and in the event of
an accident please quote your policy number. If you have
any further queries or need information on any of our other
policies please contact our Customer Service Division.

Yours sincerely


Huw Jones
Sales Director

Enc
```

Task 2 Key in the following memorandum with today's date.

```
MEMORANDUM

From    Sales Director

To      Advertising

Date    Today's

Please be informed that I shall require a full sales
promotion on our new SAFEGUARD YOUR HOME plan. A folded
brochure of the usual standard will be required together
with information packs as follows:

500 000 brochures
500 000 information packs
```

Practice Assignment 3: Unit 3 – Element 3.1

Learning Point   Complete both Tasks 1 and 2 within a ten-minute period with no more than two errors.

Task 1   Produce the following letter with an envelope.

```
Ref  TW/1p

Today's date

Mrs T Thistleboon
15 Howard View
Castleford
Yorks
CA2 7PL

Dear Mrs Thistleboon

Further to your interview with Mr Tremeyne our General
Manager and Mr Speake our Financial Secretary, we have
pleasure in offering you a position as Assistant Management
Accountant in our Harrogate Division subject to a medical
examination.

The post will carry the usual responsibilities of a senior
position and you will be directly responsible to the
Executive Team. I enclose two copies of your contract with
this Company and would be pleased if you could sign and
return one copy as soon as possible.

Congratulations and welcome aboard.

Yours sincerely


F Chambers
Personnel Officer

Enc
```

Task 2   Key in the following memorandum with today's date.

```
MEMORANDUM

From    Personnel

To      GM  FA

Date    Today's

I have offered Ms Thistleboon a Contract of Employment with
the customary conditions and have invited her to take up
the post of Assistant Financial Accountant as from the
beginning of the new financial year.
```

Practice Assignment 4: Unit 3 – Element 3.2

Learning Point Checking and marking manuscript and typewritten material with typographical, grammar, spelling, layout and calculation errors

On completion of all tasks you will be ready to put yourself forward for assessment of Element 3.2 of Unit 3 at NVQ Level 1.

Scenario You are training to become a Word Processing Supervisor and as such have been asked to check Documents 1–10 which follow.

Task 1 Check the handwritten document below before it is passed to the word processing operators: use commonly used correction signs (check in the Word Processing Section, page 5). Your supervisor has also asked you to check the figures.

Document 1

ALBLINDS MANUFACTURING Co

High quality window blinds, venetian and verticle drop. suitable for any room in the house.

We offer a custom made service with delivery and fitting within 2 week of order.

Prices as follow

Width	Height	Cost	Fitting	Sale	VAT 17½%
3'6"	3 ft	£49	£10	£59	£10.32
4'0"	3 ft	£54	£12	£64	£11.20
4'-6"	3 ft	£70	£15	£85	£14.85
5!0"	3 ft	£85	£17.50	£102.50	£17.85
6'0"	3 ft	£97	£18.25	£106.25	£18.30
3'6"	4 ft	£52	£12	£64	£11.20
4'0"	4 ft	£70	£15	£85	£14.82
4'6"	4 ft	£85	£16.25	£104.30	£18.20
5'0"	4 ft	£90	£20	£110	£19.25
6'0"	4 ft	£105	£25	£130	£22.75

Task 2   Read through the typewritten letters (Documents 2–5) and correct them using the commonly used correction signs.

Document 2

STEADMAN & HAWKINS
ESTATE AGANTS
2 Market Square
STOURBRIDGE
West Midlands

WM2 50Z

Tel 0487 876453   Faxs 0487 875349

14 Octobre 199

Miss JanetThorning
147 Ridgemont
HAGELEY
West Midlands
WM2 20H

Dear Ms Thorning

Further to your intarview with Mrs Speake, our Word
Processing Supervisor, we have pleasurein ofering yyou the
position of Word Processing Operater.

    As discussed at interview, the system you will be using
is WordPerfect and you will be directly responsible to Mrs
Speake.

Our office hours is flexible and you may work at any time
between 7.00am and 7.00 pm provided you cover a 35 hour
week. You wil have four week holiday per anum together with
statutary holidays with a salary of £8,000.

    Pleas confirm if you wish to accept this offer.

Yours Sincerly

RICHARD DENNING
personel Officer

Document 3

STEADMAN & HAWKINS
ESTATE AGANTS
2 Market Square
STOURBRIDGE
West Midlands

WM2 5OZ

Tel 0487 876453   Faxs 0487 875349

14 Octobre 199

Mis Shelly Wheldon
23 Dobbins Oak Walk
Hageley
West midlands
WM2 OTY

Dear Miss Weldon

Further to your inteview with our word Processing
Supervisor, we regret that you werr unsucesful on this
ocassion.

We would like to thank you for your interest in the
position and intend to put your name on our files should
another vaccancy ocurr.

Yours Sincerly

RICHARD DENNING
personel Officer

Document 4

```
         MELLAWEAR FITTED KITCHENS
               HODGE HOUSE
               THE STRAND
                 CARDIFF
                 CF1 2mw
```

28 oCTOBER 199

Dear customer,

KITCHENS FOR ALL

Designing a kitchen to meet individual requirements is essential to our business. A good design is not about trying to fit in as many appliances as posible but tailoring a kitchen to mete different lifestyles.

ESKIMO

White is the ideal choise if your kitchen is dark. The finnish is easy to care melamine which gives the convenience of a wipe -down surface.

DOVETAIL

A soft shade of grey with a textared vinyl surfase creates a sleak italian look to your kitchen.

CLASS OAK

designed to give a kitchen a touch of clas, these qualty units build on the real qality of oak to offer you tremendus scope whether your kitchen si lage or small.

ENGLAND

This supurb range fo units combines the 'old worlde'' charm with excelent workmanship. A comprehensi ve range of acessories is also available.

sales Manager
MELAWEAR FITTED KITCHENs

Document 5

```
IT SUPPORT SYSTEMS
FARLEY CORN EXCHANGE
FAIRHAM
HAMPSHIRE
HO2 a5tH
```

28 February 199

Dear Mr Singh

Please find below our report on software.

VALUE FOR MONY

Large organisations have financial freedum to chose sophisticated hardware and softwear wheras small busineses usuallyhave to shop around for budget priced sistems and software.

There are dplenty of choise at the cheap end of the market, with software programms for under £100 and hardware to run it on for under £1000.

Is buying cheap the way to poor quality? The answer is yes, toughness of system is esential and some cheap hardwear have poor design and flimsy casings. Cheap softwear lacks facilities or can be uncompatible with other softwear, or worse stil have, b ugs wich cause data to be lost or corupted.

After- sales support of low-grade software could even be non-existent, although some can offer grate value for money.

With the high price systems and packages come good after-sales care and can even include a feesibility study to ensur the system is just right for the organization.and sometimes, installation and training are also included.

Task 3   Check Documents 6–10 against the originals which follow each one (6a–10a). Correct these copies using the correction signs (see page 5).

Document 6

```
MEMORANDUM

From  Bill Serle (Buyer)

To    Sales

Date  Today's

The following roses are now in stock:
```

TYPE	ROSE	COLOUR	FRAGRANCE	ORDER NO
TE	Grandpa Dicksen	Yellow	SF	T01
	Pascali	White	VF	T02
	Whisky Mac	Orange	SF	T03
	Superstar	Pink	F	T04
	Silver Jubilee	Pink	SF	T06
FL	Algold	Yellow	SF	FL01
	Chinatown	Yellow	F	FL02
	Elizabeth of Glams	White	F	FL03
	Iceberg	White	SF	FL04
	Orange Sensatieon	Orange	F	FL05
	Paddy McGreedy	Pink	SF	FL06
MN	Angela Rippon	Orange	SF	MN01
	Yellow Doll	Yellow	SF	MN03
	Scarlet Gem	Red	SF	MN02
	Pour Toi	White	SF	MN04
	Little Flirt	Cerise	SF	MN05

Document 6a: Original

```
MEMORANDUM

From  Bill Searle (Buyer)

To    Sales Department

Date  Today's

The following roses are now in stock:
```

TYPE	ROSE	COLOUR	FRAGRANCE	ORDER NO
TE	Grandpa Dickson	Yellow	SF	T01
	Pascali	White	VF	T02
	Whiskey Mac	Orange	VF	T03
	Superstar	Pink	F	T04
	Silver Jubilee	Pink	SF	T06
FL	Allgold	Yellow	SF	FL01
	Chinatown	Yellow	F	FL02
	Elizabeth of Glamis	Pink	F	FL03
	Iceberg	White	SF	FL04
	Orange Sensation	Orange	F	FL05
	Paddy McGready	Pink	SF	FL06
MN	Angela Rippon	Orange	SF	MN01
	Yellow Doll	Yellow	SF	MN03
	Scarlet Gem	Red	SF	MN02
	Pour Toi	White	SF	MN04
	Little Flirt	Cerise	SF	MN05

Document 7

```
TOPS TRAINING AGENCY

ART FOR BEGINNERS                              Tutor P Crowley
A course for complete beginners

BASS GUITAR                                    Tuter R Paynton
A course for beginners, bring your
own guitar

CERAMICS                                       Tutor A Walbyoff
A course for both beginners and
intermediate students

DANISH PASTRY COURSE                           Tutor L Thomlinson
A Cordon blue course

ENGLISH (GCSE)                                 Tutor R Mole
A year long course, assessed by
course-work and written examination

FRENCH - Beginners                             Tutor E Toolittle
A Course for those wishing to know
the basic prior to visiting France

FRENCH - GCSE
A year long course, assessed by
course-work, oral and written examination
```

Document 7a: Original

```
TOPS TRAINING AGENCY

ART FOR BEGINNERS                              Tutor P Crawley
A 10-week course for complete beginners

BASS GUITAR                                    Tutor R Paynton
A course for beginners: bring your
own guitar

CERAMICS                                       Tutor A Walbyoff
A course for both beginners and
intermediate students

DANISH PASTRY COURSE                           Tutor L Tomlinson
A cordon bleu course

ENGLISH (GCSE)                                 Tutor R Mole
A year long course, assessed by
coursework, and written examination

FRENCH - Beginners                             Tutor E Toolittle
A course for those wishing to know
the basic prior to visiting France

FRENCH - GCSE
A 36-week-long course, assessed by
coursework, oral and written examination
```

Document 8

Word-Processing is the preperation of typewriten material using computers for the storage and manipulation of text. An organisation hving use for word processing facilities may instal either a dedicated word processor or a word processing package for use on a micocomputer.

In general, if word processing is the main requirement, then a dedicated system will be the best ivestment simply because it is designed only for word processing and will perform the function to a high very standard. If other applications are required, then it would be sensible to invest in a general purpose microcomputer which will run other applications too.

Improved facilities include:

Ability to correct documents before printing
Ability to produce a final document from draft simply by editing and retyping
Ability to call up from disk, standard paragraphs to boilerplate letters
Ability to merge files to produce a mailshot.

The main advantage with using a word processor is the increased productivity time, savings are estimated as follows:

	Typing time reduced by
Retyping of letters, reports etc	70%
Typing of letters using standard paragraphs	83%
Retyping of catalog lists, price lists etc	60$

Document 8a: Original

Word processing is the preparation of typewritten material using computers for the storage and manipulation of text. An organisation having use for word processing facilities may install either a dedicated word processor or a word processing package for use on a microcomputer.

In general, if word processing is the main requirement, then a dedicated system will be the best investment simply because it is designed only for word processing and will perform the function to a very high standard. If other applications are required, then it would be sensible to invest in a general purpose microcomputer which will run other applications too.

Improved facilities include:

Ability to correct documents before printing
Ability to produce a final document from draft simply by editing and retyping
Ability to call up from disk standard paragraphs to boilerplate letters
Ability to merge files to produce a mailshot.

The main advantage with using a word processor is the increased productivity time: savings are estimated as follows:

	Typing time reduced by
Retyping of letters, reports, etc	70%
Typing of letters using standard paragraphs	83%
Retyping of catalogue lists, price lists, etc	60%

Document 9

ALBLIND MANUFACTURING COMPANY

Parkhurst Estate, Salway, SL1 2TH

Tel 0496 230957   Fax 0495 23673

Urgently require

EXPERIENCED SALES PERSON

We manufacture a comprehensive range of window blinds, both venetian and vertical drop direct to the public.

Our sales representative will be required to cover Salway and the immediate surround area, including Tetworth, calling on both our existing customers and developing new contracts.

It would be advantageous to have previous sales experience but a person with the right personality and drive would be given training.

There will be a basic salary covering expenses but the bulk of earnings will be on a commission basis.

Interested persons please contact

NEVILLE LONGFORD ON 0496 230957

Document 9a: Original

ALBLIND MANUFACTURING COMPANY
Parkhurst Estate, Salway, SL1 2TH

Tel 0496 230957   Fax 0495 23673

Urgently require

EXPERIENCED SALES PERSON

We manufacture a comprehensive range of window blinds, both Venetian and vertical drop, direct to the public.

Our Sales Representative will be required to cover Salway and the immediate surrounding area, including Tetworth, calling on both our existing customers and developing new contracts.

It would be advantageous to have previous sales experience but a person with the right personality and drive will be given training.

There will be a basic salary covering expenses but the bulk of earnings will be on commission basis.

Interested ~~people~~ persons please contact

NEVILLE LONGFORD ON 0496 230957

Document 10

ALBLIND MANUFACTURING COMPANY

MAIL ORDER CDUSTOMERS

G Edwards
10 Meadow Grove
Salway
0496 23056

K Buckley
14 Treetower Court
Salway
0496 23408

T Hucklefin
15 High Beeches
Huxtely
0496 87365

J Benn
197 King Street
Tetworth
0496 76298

Mr M MacEwen
Roxbrough Avenue
Salway
0496 87294

Mr P Jason
Glanfroid Walk
Tetworth
0496 76923

P Moffat
Station House
Tetworth
0496 76838

L Morris
14 Station Terrace
Tetworth
0496 76002

T Jones
45 Cendle Crescent
Huxtley
0496 87481

K Jolly
The Chestnuts
Salway
0496 23058

Document 10a: Original

ALBLIND MANUFACTURING COMPANY

Mail order Customers —— caps

G Edwards
10 Meadow Grove
Salway
0496 23056

K Buckley
14 Treetower Court
Salway
0496 23408

T Hucklefin
15 High Beeches
Huxtley
0496 87365

J Benn
197 King Street
Tetworth
0496 76298

Mr M MacEwen
Roxbrough Avenue
Salway
0496 87294

Mr P Jason
Glanfroid Walk
Tetworth
0496 76923

P Moffat
Station House ——— Tetworth
0496 76838

L Morris
14 Station Terrace
Tetworth
0496 76002

T Jones
43 Cendle Cresc.
Huxtley
0496 87481

K Jolly
The Chestnuts
Salway
0496 23038

You are now ready to put yourself forward for assessment of NVQ Unit 3 –
Elements 3.1 and 3.2.

Practice Assignment 5: Unit 3 – Element 3.3

Notes   A more difficult version of this assignment is included in assessment for Unit 13 – Element 13.1. You may choose to do that assignment and be assessed at both levels simultaneously.

Tutors need to create a database for students to use. The material will be found on page 192.

Scenario   You are employed by an Estate Agent with three branches in South Wales. You work in the Cardiff branch but the branch computers are all linked into your office. The staff in the office are constantly asked to supply the following information:

- A selection of properties in a specific price range
- A list of properties in alphabetical order
- A list of specific type properties, e.g. semi or detached property.

A database has been created to accommodate the information listed in Task 1. (This should be keyed in by a tutor.)

In order to satisfy the NVQ assessment criteria, access to and manipulation of database need to be demonstrated on three separate occasions. For this purpose you will work in a format of three working weeks; it is recommended you start up and close down your system to separate the three occasions.

Week 1

Task 1   Recall the database file called ESTATE and key in the following 12 records, checking your screen carefully before saving data to file. Print out a copy of your database.

BRANCH ADDRESS	PROPERTY	TYPE	BED	PRICE	TENURE
SWANSEA					
23 Cefn Bryn View Oxwich	House	Detached	5	170000	F
102 Morlais Road Sketty	Bungalow	Semi	3	95500	F
29 The Kingsway Swansea	Flat		2	60500	L
23 The Marina Swansea	Flat		2	65500	F
38 Vernon Drive Killay	House	Semi	3	85000	F
24 Dunvant Park Killay	Bungalow	Detached	2	64750	F
PONTYPRIDD					
28 Arran Road Pontypridd	Bungalow	Detached	3	62950	L
59 Church Crescent Pontypridd	House	Terraced	3	64950	L
5 Windsor Avenue Quakers Yard	House	Linked	2	35500	F
24 Christopher Rise Merthyr	Bungalow	Detached	3	65000	F
CARDIFF					
27 Penarth Road Cardiff	Bungalow	Detached	3	85500	F
87 Treharan Gardens Cardiff	House	Semi	3	90950	F

Task 2   Print out a copy of the complete database and check this against the original. Correct any errors and save the database file. Print out another copy of the corrected database.

Task 3   Make up a folder to take the print-outs, label print-outs and file in correct order, i.e. first print-out appearing first.

Close down your system.

Week 2

Recall the database called ESTATE.

Task 1   This week there are a number of new properties to be added to the database. Access the database file and add the following 12 records to the database, checking your screen carefully before saving.

BRANCH ADDRESS	PROPERTY	TYPE	BED	PRICE	TENURE
SWANSEA					
Richmond Mayals Park	House	Detached	5	210000	F
2 Corporation Road Llanelli	House	Semi	3	39500	F
34 Goetre Heulwen Dunvant	Bungalow	Detached	3	85000	F
CARDIFF					
34 Cardiff Road Tonteg	House	Detached	4	75000	F
1 Birch Grove Treforest	House	Detached	3	59750	F
97 Porth Road Pontypridd	Bungalow	Detached	4	72900	F
29 High Street Taffs Well	House	Semi	3	49500	L
17 York Place Nelson	Bungalow	Semi	3	45500	F
24 Grantham Place	House	Detached	4	85950	F
188 St Mellons Drive Cardiff	Bungalow	Semi	2	78500	F
70 Vaughan Terrace Llandaff	House	Semi	4	64600	L
34 Cowbridge Road West Canton	House	Detached	5	120600	F

Task 2   Print out a copy of the whole database with additions.

Task 3   Your Manager asks you to correct two mistakes which have been made with the following properties:

- The flat on the Kingsway at Swansea is freehold and not leasehold as previously entered.
- The house at 5 Windsor Avenue, Quakers Yard is £37 500 and not £35 500 as previously entered.

Task 4   Print out a new copy of those two amended records. Save your database file and close down your system.

Week 3

Recall the database called ESTATE.

Task 1   The following properties have been taken on during the past week. You are asked to key in the details.

BRANCH ADDRESS	PROPERTY	TYPE	BED	PRICE	TENURE
SWANSEA					
36 Penlan Road Townhill	House	Terraced	2	29500	F
18 Llanrhidian Court Dunvant	Bungalow	Detached	3	95500	F
Arosfa Llanmadoc Drive Sketty	House	Detached	3	87500	L
PONTYPRIDD					
28 Llwyn Heulog Tonteg	House	Link	3	49500	F
CARDIFF					
45 Rhymney Close Canton	Bungalow	Semi	3	65500	L
129 Cefn Bridge Ely	House	Semi	4	90500	L
35 Gaer Avenue Rhymney	House	Detached	5	135000	F
Harefield Taff View Radyr	House	Detached	4	130750	F

Task 2   The Agency Manager wishes to have a print-out of all properties on the books of all branches in alphabetical order of BRANCH. Sort the database into this order and prepare a print-out.

Task 3   A potential buyer wishes to have a list of all semi-detached properties, so you are asked to print this.

Task 4   Your Manager is concerned about the loss of valuable information if the computer goes down or your work disk is damaged: format another disk and make a backup copy of your database.

Practice Assignment 6: Unit 13 – Element 13.1

Scenario   You are employed by an Estate Agent with three branches in South Wales. You work in the Cardiff branch but the branch computers are all linked into your office. The staff in the office are constantly asked to supply the following information:

- A selection of properties in a specific area.
- A selection of properties in a particular price range.
- A list of specific type properties, e.g. semi or detached property.
- A list of properties in alphabetical order of type.
- A selection of properties meeting more than one criteria.
- A selection of 3- or 4-bedroom homes.
- All freehold properties.

Note   A simplified version of this assignment is included in Unit 3 Element 3.3.

In order to satisfy the NVQ assessment criteria, access to and manipulation of database needs to be demonstrated on three separate occasions. For this purpose you will work in a format of three working weeks. It is also recommended that the system is closed down after each 'week' to simulate three separate occasions.

Week 1

Task 1   Create a database with the filename ESTATE to contain the following fields.

```
BRANCH
ADDRESS
PROPERTY
TYPE
BED
PRICE
TENURE
```

Enter the records which follow.

BRANCH ADDRESS	PROPERTY	TYPE	BED	PRICE	TENURE
SWANSEA					
198 Mayals Avenue Mumbles	House	Detached	4	165000	F
23 Cefn Bryn View Oxwich	House	Detached	5	170000	F
102 Morlais Road Sketty	Bungalow	Semi	3	95500	F
29 The Kingsway Swansea	Flat		2	60500	L
23 The Marina Swansea	Flat		2	65500	F
38 Vernon Drive Killay	House	Semi	3	85000	F
24 Dunvant Park Killay	Bungalow	Detached	2	64750	F
PONTYPRIDD					
15 Hightrees Lane Treharris	House	Semi	3	55650	F
28 Arran Road Pontypridd	Bungalow	Detached	3	62950	L
59 Church Crescent Pontypridd	House	Terraced	3	64950	L
5 Windsor Avenue Quakers Yard	House	Linked	2	35500	F
24 Christopher Rise Merthyr	Bungalow	Detached	3	65000	F
CARDIFF					
Hatherley Cefn Coed	House	Detached	5	198000	F
27 Penarth Road Cardiff	Bungalow	Detached	3	85500	F
87 Treharan Gardens Cardiff	House	Semi	3	90950	F

Task 2   Print out the database structure.

Task 3   Print out a copy of the complete database and check this against the original. Correct any errors and save the database file. Print out another copy of the corrected database if necessary.

Task 4   Search the database for properties with three bedrooms, and print out.

Task 5   Make up a folder to take the print-outs. Label the folder ESTATE AGENTS and label print-outs, filing in correct order with the first print out appearing first. Close down your system.

Week 2

Task 1   This week there are a number of new properties to be added to the database. Access the database file and add the following 12 records, checking your screen carefully before saving and printing the complete database.

BRANCH ADDRESS	PROPERTY	TYPE	BED	PRICE	TENURE
SWANSEA					
Richmond Mayals Park	House	Detached	5	210000	F
2 Corporation Road Llanelli	House	Semi	3	39500	F
34 Goetre Heulwen Dunvant	Bungalow	Detached	3	85000	F
CARDIFF					
34 Cardiff Road Tonteg	House	Detached	4	75000	F
1 Birch Grove Treforest	House	Detached	3	59750	F
97 Porth Road Pontypridd	Bungalow	Detached	4	72900	F
29 High Street Taffs Well	House	Semi	3	49500	L
17 York Place Nelson	Bungalow	Semi	3	45500	F
24 Grantham Place	House	Detached	4	85950	F
188 St Mellons Drive Cardiff	Bungalow	Semi	2	78500	F
70 Vaughan Terrace Llandaff	House	Semi	4	64600	L
34 Cowbridge Road West Canton	House	Detached	5	120600	F

Task 2   Your Manager asks you to correct two mistakes which have been made with the following properties.

a) The flat on The Kingsway at Swansea is freehold and not leasehold as previously entered

b) The house at 5 Windsor Avenue, Quakers Yard is £37 500 and not £35 500 as previously entered.

Task 3   Print out a new copy of those two amended records only. Save your database file.

Task 4 A telephone call from the Cardiff Branch reveals that

a) the property at No 1 Birch Grove, Treforest has been sold and should be removed from the database

b) the owner of Richmond at Mayals Park, Swansea has withdrawn his property, remove from database.

Task 5 Print out your complete database.

Task 6 A potential buyer wishes to view a number of semi-detached properties. Produce a list of all semi-detached properties on the books. Don't forget to file your print-outs in a correct manner and close down your system.

Week 3

The Agency Manager has left a list of new properties that he wishes you to add to the database. The Swansea Branch have typed their list but the Manager was in a rush and has handwritten the Cardiff and Pontypridd properties for you on the Swansea memo (below).

MEMORANDUM

From SWANSEA BRANCH

To CARDIFF BRANCH

Date 23 April 1992

Herewith the new properties taken on during the past week. They are all freehold.

ADDRESS	PROPERTY	TYPE	BED	PRICE
36 Penlan Road Townhill	House	Terraced	2	29,500
18 Llanrhidian Court Dunvant	Bungalow	Detached	3	95,500
Arosfa Llanmadoc Drive Sketty	House	Detached	3	87,500

Pontypridd

28 Llwyn Heulog Tonteg	House	Link	3	£49,500	F

Cardiff

45 Rhymney Close Canton	Bungalow	Semi	3	£65,500	F
129 Cefn Bridge Ely	House	Semi	4	£90,500	F
35 Gaer Avenue Rhymney	House	Detached	5	£135,000	F
Harefield Taff View Radyr	House	Detached	4	£130,750	F

Task 1 The Agency Manager wishes to have a print-out of all properties on the books of all branches in alphabetical order of BRANCH. Please sort database into this order and prepare a print-out.

Task 2   A client has requested a selection of properties in the Pontypridd area with three bedrooms under £50 000. Print out properties meeting this criteria.

Task 3   Sort the database into numerical order of price, from the cheapest to the most expensive.

Task 4   A retired businessman and his wife wish to retire to Wales and are looking for a bungalow near Cardiff. Print out a selection of properties for them.

Task 5   Your Manager is concerned about the loss of valuable information if the computer goes down or your work disk is damaged. Format another disk and make a backup copy of your database.

Task 6   A new assistant has been taken on and you have been asked to explain the database system to her. Write notes on how the above searches in Week 3 were made.

Task 7   Write a short account of the conditions of the Data Protection Act.

For a practice assignment using another commercial database, use the stock control exercise in Module 5.

Practice Assignment 7: Unit 13 – Element 13.2

Learning Point   Creating a spreadsheet
Using formulae to calculate totals of rows and columns
Forecasting, i.e. using a WHAT IF technique.

Scenario   You work in the Administration Department of your local school. For assessment purposes you will work in a format of four days. It is recommended that your system is closed down at the end of each day.

Day one

You have been asked to put the final year student examination results on a spreadsheet in order to calculate the students' total marks and position in the class.

Task 1   a)   Design and create a spreadsheet to accommodate the following.

Student	English	History	Maths	Science
Durnley Robert	65	58	76	80
Thorning Alister	75	83	72	74
Taylor Alwyn	60	69	58	54
Weed Sarah	64	65	80	84
Barton Jonathan	85	80	76	84
Tipping Rachel	83	84	59	57
Weston Alan	52	50	58	54
Ball Elizabeth	92	85	49	54
Evans Barbara	59	65	54	50
Swanton Tracey	51	50	45	48
Goodyear Lisa	50	48	50	35
Eversley Robert	60	67	70	75
Gould Philippa	58	58	35	49
James Patricia	58	65	50	51
Firkin Samantha	84	80	60	52

b)   Enter a totals column and use a suitable formula to calculate the first student's marks; replicate to produce all students' totals. Print a copy of your spreadsheet.

c)   The computer teacher has forgotten to give you the results for the class; enter the figures below and recalculate the totals.

Durnley Robert	Thorning Alister	Taylor Alwyn	Weed Sarah
60	58	39	69
Barton Jonathan	**Tipping Rachel**	**Weston Alan**	**Ball Elizabeth**
80	65	58	80
Evans Barbara	**Swanton Tracey**	**Goodyear Lisa**	**Eversley Robert**
57	54	39	58
Gould Philippa	**James Patricia**	**Firkin Samantha**	
70	52	75	

d)   Sort the spreadsheet so that the students are in alphabetical order of name.

e)   Print a copy of the spreadsheet.

Task 2   The Headmaster has asked for the average mark of the class and also needs, for review purposes, the average mark for each subject.

a) Recall your spreadsheet and add a column for AVERAGE MARK; use a formula to determine the average mark for the first student. Replicate for all students.

b) Sort the spreadsheet on AVERAGE MARK to determine the student position in the class.

c) Add a totals row to add up all marks awarded for each subject; use a suitable formula to calculate totals.

d) Insert another row AVERAGE MARK and use a formula to calculate the average mark for each subject.

e) Print out a copy of your spreadsheet, displaying all figures as integers.

f) Rachel Tipping normally has a high mark for computing. Use a WHAT IF technique to determine her class position if she had 85 instead of 65.

e) Print another copy of the spreadsheet showing the new figures.

Day two

The Headmaster wishes to have the whole school's subject results ready for a Governors' Meeting.

Task 1   a) Design and create a spreadsheet to accommodate the following data.

Subject	Year 1	Year 2	Year 3	Year 4	Year 5
ENGLISH	60	57	52	60	70
HISTORY	59	58	49	51	58
MATHEMATICS	56	58	50	52	60
SCIENCE	50	53	59	60	63
COMPUTING	49	54	56	60	60
FRENCH	50	50	52	54	58
GERMAN	51	52	50	56	56
RELIGIOUS STUDIES	56	54	56	60	62

b) Add a TOTALS column to determine the total marks for English and replicate the formula to determine all subjects.

c) Add a TOTALS row to determine totals for Year 1; replicate to total all other years.

d) Print a copy of your spreadsheet and save.

Task 2   a) Recall your spreadsheet and add a TOTAL AVERAGE row; use a suitable formula to determine the year average. Replicate the formula to determine the other year's total averages to two decimal places.

b) Recall your spreadsheet and add a OVERALL AVERAGE column; use a suitable formula to determine the overall average mark for English. Replicate the formula to determine averages for all other subjects.

c) Print a copy of your spreadsheet.

d) If the average Computing mark in Year 1 had been 60 and not 49, by how much would the whole school average alter?

e) Print a copy of the projected figures and save your spreadsheet.

Day three

The Headmaster requires a detailed list of stationery costs used by all departments during the month of January.

Task 1

a) Design and create a spreadsheet to accommodate the following figures.

	Lined Paper	Pens/ Pencils	Printer Ribbons	Listing Paper	Box Files	Ring Binders
ENGLISH	25.00	9.60	3.45	15.00	30.00	30.00
MATHEMATICS	23.50	5.60	3.45	15.00	26.80	15.00
HISTORY	22.60	6.25	3.45	15.00	30.00	16.00
SCIENCE	25.00	9.60	3.45	15.00	25.00	15.00
COMPUTING	8.50	2.56	35.00	50.00	1.50	15.00

b) Add a column for departmental totals; use a formula to calculate the total for the English Department and replicate to calculate all other departmental totals.

c) Add a row for item totals; use a formula to calculate the total lined paper used and replicate that formula to calculate all totals.

d) The Headmaster needs to have an approximate overall total of all usage for a year. Taking a year to be 10 months, add a GRAND TOTAL column and use a formula to project these estimated figures.

Day four

You have been asked to put the departmental stationery costs on a spreadsheet to calculate the actual usage over the past six months and project new figures for the coming year.

Task 1

a) Design and create a spreadsheet to accommodate the following figures.

	JAN £	FEB £	MAR £	APR £	MAY £	JUNE £
ENGLISH	95.60	123.68	95.59	102.00	105.20	135.45
HISTORY	86.56	93.00	89.50	100.35	125.50	145.50
MATHEMATICS	75.59	85.00	73.35	80.50	95.65	120.50
SCIENCE	58.75	69.75	74.25	72.25	78.59	100.73
COMPUTING	98.50	96.25	99.99	105.60	130.45	150.36

b) Enter a totals column and use a formula to total costs for the English Department. Replicate that formula for the other departments.

c) Add a totals row and use a formula to total monthly usage for January; replicate for other months.

d) Sort the spreadsheet into alphabetical order of department. Print a copy of your completed spreadsheet and save your spreadsheet.

Task 2

a) Recall your spreadsheet and delete the totals column.

Add further columns to include July, September, October, November, December. The usage for these columns is identical to those from February to June; use a formula to copy each department's usage for those months.

b) Enter a YEARLY TOTAL column and use a formula to calculate the total of the English Department. Replicate to calculate totals of the other department.

c) Print out a copy of the spreadsheet.

d) The Science Department are planning to take on a project which will double their stationery usage for the month of October. The only problem is funding. Project this new total to see how much the yearly total will be affected.

Print out one copy and save the spreadsheet.

RSA CLAIT ASSIGNMENTS

Tutor information

It is recommended that tutors test the assignments in this section before they are used

a) to check whether they need to be adapted for the hard/software students will be using,
b) to ensure the terminology used is understood by their students.

RSA CLAIT Word Processing Assignment 1

1.1.1	**1**	Load your word processing program.
1.1.2	**2**	Key in the text below with an UNJUSTIFIED right-hand margin. Call your file RSA1.

THE ADVANTAGES OF ENGINE TUNING

Complaints made by car owners indicating that tuning is necessary are: petrol consumption; misfiring, sluggish engine; poor acceleration; hard starting. In recommending a tuning for such complaints the service mechanic should remember that the owner is entitled to know what is proposed and how much it is all going to cost.

The average car owner will probably have some theory concerning poor performance, and he expects the mechanic to diagnose a definite remedy.

It should be explained, however, that the cause of poor performance is the gradual change of the adjustment settings built into the engine, and what is necessary is to restore all these. These adjustments to their original settings, may, or may not, involve new parts or reconditioning of old parts.

1.4.1	**3**	Save your file.
	4	Print one copy.
1.4.2	**5**	Reload your file and amend as follows.
1.1.1	**6**	In the second sentence insert the word 'any' after 'for' and before 'such complaints'.
1.2.4	**7**	a) In the second paragraph replace the words 'will probably have some theory' with 'may have some ideas'.
		b) In the second paragraph change the word 'poor' to 'low'.
1.2.2	**8**	Delete the third paragraph.
1.2	**9**	Add the following paragraph to appear as the second paragraph.
	10	No service mechanic can give a car owner any real service by accepting instructions to 'clean plugs', 'adjust carburettor', etc. Regardless of what the owner thinks he needs to have done, what he really wants and expects to have is a return of good performance.
1.3.1	**11**	Reformat both margins to reduce the width of the document by five spaces from both left and right margins.
1.3.2, 1.33	**12**	JUSTIFY the whole document except for the second paragraph which is to be UNJUSTIFIED and in DOUBLE SPACING.
1.3.4, 1.3.5	**13**	Centre and embolden the main heading.
1.2.3	**14**	Change the order of the third and fourth paragraphs.
1.4.1, 1.4.2	**15**	Save your file and print a copy.
1.4.3	**16**	Exit from program.

RSA CLAIT Word Processing Assignment 2

1.1.1   **1**   Load your word processing program.

1.1.2   **2**   Key in the text below with an UNJUSTIFIED right-hand margin and call your file RSA3.

```
LIFE SAVING

Water must always be treated with respect, otherwise
it can kill! Safety is most important in all swimming
activities and someone qualified in life-saving
techniques must always be present.

The swimming teacher's ability to life-save is of
paramount importance. The teacher should learn the
skills of life-saving thoroughly and should practise
them regularly. The most important aspect of a life-
saver is that they must be an accomplished swimmer. It
is no good trying to save some poor person in
difficulties if you cannot swim yourself. Teaching
qualifications demand that teachers have some life-
saving ability.

Water fitness is also very important. Knowing the
principles of life-saving and being able to life-save
are two very different things. Being fit in water is
achieved in only one way, and that is by regular
swimming and practising of life-saving skills.
```

1.4.1   **3**   Save your file.

1.4.2   **4**   Print one copy.

1.1.1   **5**   Reload your file and amend as follows.

1.2.1   **6**   In the first sentence insert the word 'great' after 'with' and before 'respect'.

1.2.2   **7**   Delete the second sentence in the first paragraph.

1.2.4   **8**   a)   In the first sentence of the second paragraph replace the words 'of paramount importance' with 'essential'.

1.2.2   **9**   Delete the third paragraph.

1.2.1   **10**   Add the following paragraph to appear as the second paragraph.

      11   In a real situation, a drowning person will attempt to grab at anything he can; once he has grasped it, he will not let go easily. Therefore it is essential not to swim straight up to the drowning person but to hold back. You may need to reassure the victim; your explanation of what is necessary may be sufficient to calm him. Always be prepared for sudden lunges and make sure you are well in control of the situation.

1.3.2   **12**   Reformat both margins to reduce the width of the document by five spaces from both left and right margins.

1.3.4, 1.3.5   **13**   Centre and embolden the main heading, LIFE SAVING.

1.3.3   **14**   JUSTIFY the whole document except for the first paragraph which is to be UNJUSTIFIED and in DOUBLE SPACING.

1.2.3   **15**   Change the order of the third and fourth paragraphs.

1.4.1, 1.4.2   **16**   Save and print a copy.

1.4.3   **17**   Exit from program.

177

RSA CLAIT Database Assignment 1

2.1.1   **1**   Power up your system and load your database program.

2.1.2   **2**   Create a database file named DBASE2 to contain fields as follows.

```
FIELD TITLE

NAME
STREET
TOWN
POSTCODE
PRICE
TENURE    L = Leasehold
          F = Freehold
TYPE      SE = Semi detached
          DE = Detached
          TE = Terraced
          LI = Link
```

2.1.3   **3**   Enter the following data.

	NAME	STREET	TOWN	POSTCODE	PRICE	TYPE
Freehold						
	Jones	15 High Street	Newport	NP1 3TH	59500	DE
	Lewis	23 The Ridge	Newport	NP5 50D	35000	DE
	Dobbs	4 Hightrees	Newport	NP4 50D	79500	DE
	Fetherho	The Knoll	Malpas	NP8 4TD	95000	DE
	Thomas	The Manse Pill	Newport	NP2 3TD	82500	DE
	Stirling	6 Commerce Street	Newport	NP3 2DE	45000	SE
	Firly	56 Malpas Road	Newport	NP7 50D	150000	DE
	Thompson	12 Chepstow Road	Maindee	NP3 9TH	39500	LI
	Rhodes	7 Larch Grove	Malpas	NP8 4TD	89500	DE
	Sempler	23 Malpas Drive	Newport	NP8 6TD	37000	SE
	Wilson	350 Chepstow Road	Maindee	NP3 9TH	37950	LI
	Sadler	The Rhyddings	Newport	NP4 5TD	45000	SE
Leasehold						
	Jenkins	8 Tudor Close	Newport	NP2 3TH	39500	LI
	Samson	25 Chepstow Road	Maindee	NP3 2DE	37500	TE
	Ronson	12 Lisvane Terr.	Newport	NP4 50D	59000	SE
	Lawson	59 Ringland Close	Newport	NP2 3TD	65600	DE
	Treddle	259 Malpas Road	Newport	NP7 60D	85000	DE
	Swansea	23 Commercial Road	Newport	NP1 2TH	38500	TE
	Watson	4 Bassaleg Road	Newport	NP5 3TH	78000	SE
	Davies	45 High Cross	Newport	NP4 5TH	85000	DE
	Arnold	359 Chepstow Road	Newport	NP3 9TH	35000	TE
	Pensom	24 Allt-yr-Yn	Newport	NP9 5TD	85500	DE
	Richards	23 Cherry Tree Av	Malpas	NP8 4TD	37500	LI

2.3.2   **4**   Sort the file chronologically in ascending order of price. Save and print.

2.2.1   **5**   Recall your file and make corrections as follows.

```
Mr Treddle's house is worth £79500
Mrs Pensom lives at 25 Allt-yr-Yn
Mr Lawson lives at Ringland Ridge not Close
Watson's house is freehold not leasehold
```

2.2.2   **6**   Add the following records.

Snowdon	15 Ridgeway	Newport	NP9 4TH	49500	DE
Philips	37 Caer Bryn	Newport	NP3 50D	35000	LI

2.2.3	**7**	Delete the record for Mr Arnold: the house has been sold.
2.3.3	**8**	Search the database for all houses in Malpas and print a list.
2.3.4, 2.3.5, 2.4.2	**9**	Reload your file and search your database for those freehold detached houses over £75 000. Print out TOWN, TYPE and PRICE field only.
2.3.1	**10**	List your database in alphabetic order of name and print your database.
2.4.1, 2.4.3	**11**	Save your database and exit from the system.

RSA CLAIT Database Assignment 2

2.1.1   **1**   Power up your system and load your database program.

2.1.2   **2**   Create a database file named DBASE3 to contain fields as follows.

```
FIELD TITLE

NAME
GROUP
YEAR
ENGLISH
MATHS
SCIENCE
LANGUAGES
```

2.1.3   **3**   Enter the following details.

NAME	GROUP	YEAR	ENGLISH	MATHS	SCIENCE	LANG
Davies Jason	4A	1991	B	A	A	B
Arnold Lucy	4B	1992	A	A	C	A
Turley David	4A	1992	C	C	C	C
Winter Susan	4A	1991	B	C	C	A
Reynolds Kim	4A	1992	A	B	B	A
White Timothy	4B	1992	C	A	A	C
Snell Lorraine	4A	1991	C	C	C	C
Patel Nadina	4B	1992	C	A	A	C
Singh Padmesh	4A	1992	C	A	A	B
Harris Lucretia	4B	1991	A	A	A	A
Arden Stephen	4A	1992	B	A	A	C
Snowdon Richard	4B	1991	A	A	A	A
Morris Linford	4B	1991	C	C	B	C
Hamley Damien	4B	1991	A	A	A	B

2.3.1, 2.4.2   **4**   Sort the file alphabetically on students' names, save and print.

2.2.1   **5**   Recall your file and make corrections as follows.

```
Kim Reynolds had a C in Maths and Science.
Lorraine Snell had an A grade in English.
Damien Hamley was in group 4A.
Jason Davies was in group 4B.
```

2.2.2   **6**   Add the following records.

```
Belinda Thomas was in group 4A in 1992 and had the
following grades: English A, Maths B, Science B, and
Languages C.
```

```
Theresa Weston was in group 4B in 1991 with the
following grades: English B, Maths C, Science C,
Languages A.
```

2.2.3   **7**   Delete the records for Linford Morris and Susan Winter.

2.3.3   **8**   Search the database for all students with an A grade in Maths and print a list.

2.3.4, 2.3.5, 2.4.2   **9**   Reload your file and search your database for students in 4A in 1992 and print out NAME and CLASS only.

2.3.2, 2.4.2   **10**   List your database in numerical order of year and print.

2.4.1, 2.4.3   **11**   Save your file and exit from program.

RSA CLAIT Spreadsheet Assignment 1

3.1.1	**1**	Load your spreadsheet program.
3.1.2	**2**	Enter the heading Salesmen.
3.1.2, 3.3.1	**3**	Starting in the second column enter the following column headings right-justified:

JANUARY FEBRUARY MARCH APRIL MAY JUNE

| 3.1.2, 3.3.1 | **4** | In the first column enter the salesmen's names left-justified. |

```
DAVIES J
DANIELS W
PHILIPS P
PEACH J
HUGHES C
JONES A
COX F
```

| 3.3.2 | **5** | Enter the data shown below with months keyed in full. Widen columns where necessary. |

NAME	JAN	FEB	MAR	APRIL	MAY	JUNE
DAVIES	28.85	39.87	23.68	38.75	40.50	39.80
DANIELS	28.76	29.85	38.57	29.98	39.60	39.75
PHILIPS	29.75	45.30	35.76	39.50	29.98	49.50
PEACH	50.50	30.68	45.60	32.97	39.60	34.50
HUGHES	39.50	36.58	45.50	39.68	41.00	34.50
JONES	40.30	34.69	58.60	48.50	24.50	24.68
COX	39.50	39.87	45.30	39.60	35.60	35.09

3.4.1, 3.4.2	**6**	Save your spreadsheet and print a copy.
3.1.1	**7**	Recall your spreadsheet and make the following corrections.
3.2.1		The January entry for Hughes should show 41.50.
		The April entry for Jones should show 49.50.
3.2.1	**8**	Delete the entry for Cox.
3.2.2	**9**	Use a formula to calculate the January monthly total.
3.2.4	**10**	Use the replicate or duplicate facility to copy the formulae for the other months.
3.4.1, 3.4.2	**11**	Save and print your spreadsheet showing formulae.
3.2.3	**12**	Add a new salesman as follows, between Peach and Hughes.

KEAN G   34.60   56.00   45.60   29.80   35.78   39.86

3.3.3	**13**	Change the format of the numeric cells to integer.
3.2.2	**14**	Insert a TOTALS column for each salesman.
3.2.2	**15**	Use a formulae to calculate all salesmen's totals and grand total of all sales.
3.3.3	**16**	Change the format of cells back to two decimal points.
3.4.1, 3.4.2	**17**	Save and print your spreadsheet showing cell values.
3.4.3	**18**	Close down system.

RSA CLAIT Spreadsheet Assignment 2

3.1.1	**1**	Load your spreadsheet program.
3.1.2	**2**	Enter the heading Salesmen.
3.1.2, 3.3.1, 3.3.2	**3**	Starting in the second column enter the following column headings left-justified. Widen columns as necessary.

```
DIGESTIVE  MARIE  MALTED MILK  CREAMS  BOURBONS
```

3.1.2, 3.3.1	**4**	In the first column enter the chain stores, left-justified.

```
FINE FARE
TESCO
CO-OP
SUPERSAVE
SAFEWAY
GATEWAY
```

3.3.3, 3.1.3	**5**	Enter the data shown below. The amounts should be to two decimal places.

```
          DIGESTIVE  MARIE   MALTED MILK  CREAMS  BOURBONS

FINEFARE   115.00    117.00  113.00       118.00  110.00
TESCO      118.00    115.00  119.00       113.00   80.00
CO-OP      110.00    118.00  112.00       119.00  112.00
SUPERSAVE   70.00     80.00  110.00       113.00  111.00
SAFEWAY    120.00    123.00  123.00       127.00  121.00
GATEWAY    112.00    113.00  115.00       114.00  112.00
```

3.4.1, 3.4.2	**6**	Save your spreadsheet and print a copy.
3.1.1	**7**	Recall your spreadsheet and make the following corrections.
3.2.1	**8**	The entry for Digestive biscuits by Tesco is 123.00; the entry for Cream biscuits for Gateway should be 120.00.
3.2.1	**9**	Delete the entry for Supersave.
3.2.2	**10**	Use a formula to calculate the total Digestive column. Duplicate facility to calculate the rest of the columns.
3.4.1, 3.4.2	**11**	Save and print your spreadsheet.
3.2.3	**12**	Add a new supermarket chain as follows, before Safeway:

```
           DIGESTIVE  MARIE   MALTED MILK  CREAMS  BOURBONS
QUICKSAVE  105.00     123.00  115.65       126.76  123.45
```

3.3.3	**13**	Change the format of the numeric cells to integer.
3.2.2	**14**	Insert a Totals column for each supermarket chain
3.2.2, 3.2.4	**15**	Use a formula to calculate the supermarket total and replicate to calculate all totals and a grand total.
3.4.2	**16**	Print your spreadsheet showing formulae used.
3.3.3	**17**	Change the cell format back to two decimal places.
3.4.1, 3.4.2	**18**	Save and print your spreadsheet.
3.4.3	**19**	Close down system.

RSA CLAIT Graphics Assignment 1

Part 1

4.1.1   **1**   Load your graph program.

4.1.2   **2**   Refer to the plan of an office as shown below. Draw the office plan.

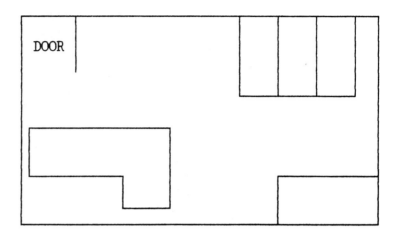

4.1.2, 4.4.1   **3**   The office has one L-shaped desk, three filing cabinets and a printer table. Design the outline shapes for each of these and store them.

4.1.3   **4**   Position the shapes within the office and label them.

4.4.2   **5**   Print out your drawing.

4.2.4   **6**   Replace the shaped desk with a rectangular desk.

4.3.1, 4.3.2   **7**   Fill in the filing cabinets with a pattern.

4.2.3   **8**   Take out the typist's chair.

4.4.2   **9**   Print out your drawing.

4.2.1   **10**   Copy the printer table shape and position it between the filing cabinets and the door.

4.3.3, 4.2.2   **11**   Rotate the original printer table and reduce it in size.

4.4.2, 4.4.3   **12**   Print your drawing and exit program.

RSA CLAIT Stock Control Assignment 1

1   Load your stock control program. Format a disk or select an empty user area.

7.1.1, 7.1.2, 7.1.3   **2**   Set up a file to record the following stock items. Initialise your system or enter any information necessary to your own system. Check with your tutor.

```
Code                B100
Description         A4 Binder
Unit Quantity      1
Re-order Level     10
Re-order Quantity  20
No in stock        23
Retail Price       1.29    (£)  Cost Price 75p

Code                B101
Description         Foolscap binder
Unit Quantity      1
Re-order Level     10
Re-order Quantity  20
No in stock        14
Retail Price       2.59    (£)  Cost Price £1.25

Code                B102
Description         Box file
Unit Quantity      1
Re-order Level     5
Re-order Quantity  5
No in stock        9
Retail Price       2.69    (£)  Cost Price £1.35

Code                W100
Description         Wallets
Unit Quantity      10
Re-order Level     10
Re-order Quantity  10
No in stock        12
Retail Price       4.48    (£)  Cost Price £2.50

Code                F100
Description         Clear folders
Unit Quantity      10
Re-order Level     10
Re-order Quantity  15
No in stock        15
Retail Price       3.89    (£)  Cost Price £1.95

Code                F101
Description         Manilla folders
Unit Quantity      100
Re-order Level     5
Re-order Quantity  10
No in stock        4
Retail Price       8.79    (£)  Cost Price £4.40

Code                F102
Description         Spring files
Unit Quantity      1
Re-order Level     10
Re-order Quantity  15
No in stock        20
Retail Price       0.49    (pence) Cost Price 25p
```

```
Code                F103
Description         Suspension files
Unit Quantity      50
Re-order Level     10
Re-order Quantity  20
No in stock        15
Retail Price       19.95   (£)  Cost Price £9.50

Code                F104
Description         Lever Arch files
Unit Quantity      1
Re-order Level     10
Re-order Quantity  15
No in stock        3
Retail Price       2.59    (£)  Cost Price £1.25

Code                T100
Description         Tippex© liquid
Unit Quantity      1
Re-order Level     25
Re-order Quantity  20
No in stock        15
Retail Price       0.56    (pence)  Cost Price 25p

Code                S100
Description         Sellotape©
Unit Quantity      1
Re-order Level     20
Re-order Quantity  25
No in stock        13
Retail Price       0.51    (pence)  Cost Price 25p

Code                S101
Description         Scotch© magic tape
Unit Quantity      1
Re-order Level     15
Re-order Quantity  10
No in stock        13
Retail Price       0.75    (pence)  Cost Price 35p
```

7.4.2   **3**   Load the printer with paper and set to the top of form. Print out a full stock list.

7.1.3, 7.2.2   **4**   Add the following three new items to your stock list.

```
Code                C100
Description         Paper clips
Unit Quantity      box
Re-order Level     5
Re-order Quantity  5
No in stock        10
Retail Price       1.45    (£)  Cost Price 75p

Code                C101
Description         Bulldog clips
Unit Quantity      10
Re-order Level     5
Re-order Quantity  5
No in stock        13
Retail Price       1.15    (£)  Cost Price 60p
```

```
Code                0100
Description         Overhead transparencies
Unit               box
Re-order level      5
Re-order quantity   5
No in stock         7
Retail price       9.85 (£) Cost price £6.50
```

7.2.1   **5**   Make the following corrections.

```
S100 - price increase to 0.55 pence.
Lever arch files are now £2.65 each.
```

7.2.3   **6**   Delete the record for Stock Code S101 as it is no longer available.

7.1.4   **7**   Issue the following stock.

```
5 × S100 and 20 F103
```

7.3.2   **8**   Print out two summary reports:
           a)   Re-order level of stock below re-order level
           b)   Value of stock of all stock.

7.4.1, 7.4.3   **9**   Save your stock file and exit from system.

RSA CLAIT VIDEOTEX Assignment 1

NOTE Tutors need to create a VIEWDATA file, using the information on page 191.

11.1.1   **1**   Log on to your VIEWDATA system, which has been set up by 'Rosea Gardens'.

11.3.1   **2**   Find the page on red hybrid tea roses; note the code and the cheapest rose.

         3   a)   What is the price of the most expensive miniature/patio rose in pink?
             b)   Find the telephone number for placing orders.

11.2.1, 11.2.2   **4**   Make up the page below using colour and background filling.

         Display 'Rosea Gardens' in double height characters in a different colour to other text.

         Make the word 'new' in line 3 flash.

         Use graphics to design background filling beneath the words SPECIALIST ROSE GROWER. Print out.

```
        *** ROSEA GARDENS ***
        SPECIALIST ROSE GROWER

        NEW CLIMBER/RAMBLER SECTION

        SPECIAL OFFERS! LOW PRICES
    ORDER NOW   NEW DISEASE-FREE STOCK

      *** PRESS 0 FOR MAIN MENU ***
```

11.3.1, 11.4.1   **5**   Save this as page 15 on the database, routeing it back to page 1.

         6   On page 1 add another item to the menu.

```
        (5) Climbers/Ramblers
```

11.1.2, 11.3.2, 11.4.1   **7**   Amend the routeing of page 1 to access the newly created page.

11.4.2   **8**   Log off or close down the system.

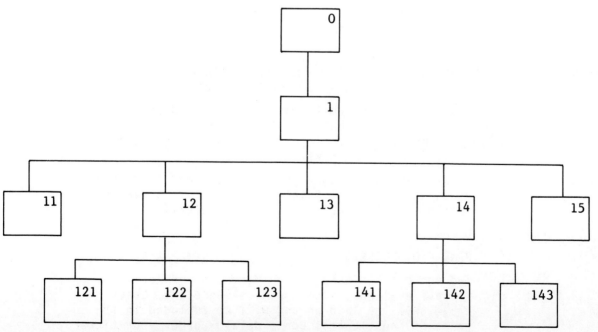

Figure 30   Illustration of routeing structure

RSA CLAIT Desktop Publishing Assignment 1

5.1.2   **1**   From the information given below, plan a layout incorporating two columns and a page-wide heading. See the suggested frame layout below.

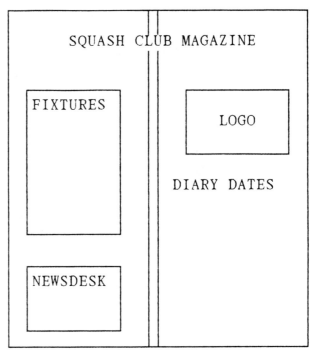

Figure 31

    2   Prepare the following text on a word processor.

```
SQUASH CLUB MAGAZINE

FIXTURES                 January-March

Nash v Ludlow            January 21
Nash v Petersfield       March 28

Nash/Ludlow              At home

Singles                  Anne-Marie Stokes
                         Judith Scrivens

Doubles                  Sigourney Frere
                         Christopher Bean
```

```
NEWSDESK  Fleur and Thomas have been chosen to
represent the club at the Squash Club of Britain
Tournament in July of this year. Well done both of you
- get in training now!

We all send our condolences to Nicky who is presently
residing in Ward B1 Royal Hospital since breaking her
leg in a riding accident. Cheer up Nicky!

Dates for your diary

BAND AID CONCERTS

Two concerts in London - on March 25 and April 13.
Tickets available from the Club Secretary. Coach
travel will be laid on and will be included in the
price of the tickets. Don't delay - order your ticket
today!
```

5.1.1	**3**	Load your desktop publisher program.
5.1.2	**4**	Set up page drawing a box for each portion of text or alternatively draw border/box when text is in place.
5.1.3	**5**	Load your previously prepared text.
	6	Select a style of HEADLINE or MAIN HEADING for the heading SQUASH CLUB MAGAZINE.
5.2.2	**7**	Centre the main heading.
5.2.6	**8**	Position the text within the frames, i.e. Fixtures will need to be placed in the framework in the first column; alternatively, draw a border/box.
5.2.4, 5.3.1	**9**	Highlight the words Fixtures January–March and use a print size of say, 16, and with COURIER, or similar font.
5.2.4, 5.3.1	**10**	Highlight the rest of the fixtures text using a print size of say, 14, and HELVETICA, or similar font.
5.2.4, 5.3.1	**11**	Using the mouse and editing tools, highlight the NEWSDESK text and position in its frame; alternatively, draw a box/border when the text is in place. Insert a new line to separate the heading from the rest of the text and use a SUBHEADING style, with print size of, say, 18 with COURIER or similar font.
5.2.6	**12**	Draw a box approximately 2" × 2" for the Squash Club logo. This should be in the right-hand column opposite the fixtures item.
	13	Position the fourth item under the logo with a SUBHEADING style centered in the column. Use the same print size and font as for the Fixtures text.
	14	Highlight the rest of the text. It should have the same print size and font as the previous text.
5.2.1	**15**	Add the following text to the newsdesk item.

It happens to the best people.

	16	Print a copy using a serif font type.
	17	Save your file.
5.2.3, 5.3.2	**18**	Recall your file but change the size of the box for the logo, and make the following changes. The text in the NEWSDESK and BAND AID CONCERT items should be justified. Using text editing functions, highlight and right-justify the text.
5.1.4	**19**	Import a previously designed picture for the LOGO section (this can be an existing package drawing), and place in position.
5.4.1, 5.4.2, 5.4.3, 5.2.5	**20**	Print your completed page, save your file and close down your system.

TUTOR SECTION

Information to be keyed in by tutors for Viewdata Exercise 2 – in Module 4 on page 129

Page 0

```
              UNITED KINGDOM

         1. Northern Ireland
         2. Wales
         3. Scotland
         4. England

         *** PRESS A NUMBER ***
```

Page 1

```
              NORTHERN IRELAND

                        1             2
County          ANTRIM        LONDONDERRY
Population      720000        180000
Principal Town  Belfast       Londonderry
Population      390000        56000

         *** PRESS 0 FOR MAIN MENU ***
```

Page 2

```
                   WALES

                     1             2
County           GWENT         POWYS
Population       470000        60000
Principal Town   Newport       Brecon
Population       110000        6470

         *** PRESS 0 FOR MAIN MENU ***
```

Page 3

```
                  SCOTLAND

                     1             2
County           ANGUS         MIDLOTHIAN
Population       280000        600000
Principal Town   Dundee        Edinburgh
Population       182000        464764

         *** PRESS 0 FOR MAIN MENU ***
```

Page 4

```
                  ENGLAND

         1. NORTHERN COUNTIES

         2. SOUTHERN

         *** PRESS 0 FOR MAIN MENU ***
```

Page 11

NORTHERN IRELAND

ANTRIM

```
Area (acres)                          720000
Population Density (acres)              0.64
Agriculture  cereals, root crops, flax
Industry  shipbuilding and container trade
```

*** PRESS 0 FOR MAIN MENU ***

Page 12

NORTHERN IRELAND

LONDONDERRY

```
Area (acres)                          530000
Population Density (acres)              0.34
Agriculture  dairy and general farming
Industry  synthetic fibres and fibres
```

*** PRESS 0 FOR MAIN MENU ***

Page 41

ENGLAND

NORTHERN COUNTIES

	1	2
County	Lancashire	Staffordshire
Population	5000000	2000000
Principal Town	Liverpool	Stoke-on-Trent
Population	660000	270000

*** PRESS 0 FOR MAIN MENU ***

Page 42

ENGLAND

SOUTHERN COUNTIES

County	Hampshire	Oxfordshire
Population	1600000	400000
Principal Town	Portsmouth	Oxford
Population	215000	110000

*** PRESS 0 FOR MAIN MENU ***

Page 421

ENGLAND

HAMPSHIRE

```
Area (acres)                          965000
Population Density (acres)              1.62
Agriculture  cattle, sheep farming, cereal crops
Industry  general engineering, boat building,
          aircraft manufacture
```

*** PRESS 0 FOR MAIN MENU ***

Page 421

ENGLAND

OXFORDSHIRE

Area (acres)	480000
Population Density (acres)	0.79
Agriculture cereal, dairy farming	
Industry car manufacture, light engineering, printing, etc.	

Database structure to be created by tutor for Unit 3 – Element 3.3 Practice Assignment on page 164

Database name   ESTATE

Structure

Fieldname	Type	Length
BRANCH	Character	10
ADDRESS	Character	30
PROPERTY	Character	8
TYPE	Character	8
BED	Numeric	1
PRICE	Numeric	10
TENURE	Character	1

BRANCH	ADDRESS	PROPERTY	TYPE	BEDROOMS	PRICE	TENURE
SWANSEA	198 Mayals Avenue Mumbles	House	Detached	4	165 000	F
PONTYPRIDD	15 Hightrees Lane Treharris	House	Semi	3	55 650	F
CARDIFF	Hatherley Cefn	House	Detached	5	198 000	F

Information to be keyed in by tutors for CLAIT VIDEOTEX Assignment on page 187

Page 0

*** ROSEA GARDENS ***

SPECIALIST ROSE GROWER

THE BEST IN THE WEST

*** PRESS 0 TO CONTINUE ***

Page 1

*** ROSEA GARDENS ***
SPECIALIST ROSE GROWER

1) Orders
2) Hybrid tea
3) Floribunda
4) Miniature /patio

PRESS A NUMBER OF YOUR CHOICE

*** PRESS 0 FOR LAST MENU ***

Page 11

```
          *** ROSEA GARDENS ***
          SPECIALIST ROSE GROWER

            TO ORDER CALL US ON
                0594 222666
        ORDERS OVER £15 DELIVERED FREE
        OTHERWISE ADD £2.00 DELIVERY
           CARD NUMBER ACCEPTED

        *** PRESS 0 FOR LAST MENU ***
```

Page 12

```
          *** ROSEA GARDENS ***
          SPECIALIST ROSE GROWER

               HYBRID TEA

              1) Pink
              2) White
              3) Red

        PRESS A NUMBER OF YOUR CHOICE

        *** PRESS 0 FOR LAST MENU ***
```

Page 13

```
          *** ROSEA GARDENS ***
          SPECIALIST ROSE GROWER

               FLORIBUNDA

              1) Pink
              2) White
              3) Red

        PRESS A NUMBER OF YOUR CHOICE

        *** PRESS 0 FOR LAST MENU ***
```

Page 14

```
          *** ROSEA GARDENS ***
          SPECIALIST ROSE GROWER

             MINIATURE/PATIO

              1) Pink
              2) White
              3) Red

        PRESS A NUMBER OF YOUR CHOICE

        *** PRESS 0 FOR LAST MENU ***
```

Page 15

```
          *** ROSEA GARDENS ***
          SPECIALIST ROSE GROWER
```

```
        PRESS A NUMBER OF YOUR CHOICE
```

Page 121

```
           *** ROSEA GARDENS ***
           SPECIALIST ROSE GROWER

                 HYBRID TEA
      Pinks in stock
      Code    Type              Scent    Price
      HT561   Superstar         F        £2.75
      HT701   Silver Jubilee    SF       £3.00
      HT493   Mischief          SF       £2.50

           *** PRESS 0 FOR LAST MENU ***
```

Page 122

```
           *** ROSEA GARDENS ***
           SPECIALIST ROSE GROWER

                 HYBRID TEA
      White in stock
      Code    Type              Scent    Price
      HT242   Pascali           VF       £2.50
      HT267   Virgo             F        £3.00

           *** PRESS 0 FOR LAST MENU ***
```

Page 123

```
           *** ROSEA GARDENS ***
           SPECIALIST ROSE GROWER

                 HYBRID TEA
      Reds in stock
      Code    Type              Scent    Price
      HT811   Ernest H Morse    VF       £2.50
      HT776   Alec's Red        F        £3.00
      HT830   Josephine         VF       £3.50

           *** PRESS 0 FOR LAST MENU ***
```

Page 141

```
           *** ROSEA GARDENS ***
           SPECIALIST ROSE GROWER

               MINIATURE/PATIO
      Pinks in stock
      Code    Type                Scent    Price
      MP115   Little Flirt        SF       £2.75
      MP209   Judy Fischer        SF       £3.00
      MP152   Perle de Monserrat  SF       £3.25

           *** PRESS 0 FOR LAST MENU ***
```

Page 142

```
           *** ROSEA GARDENS ***
           SPECIALIST ROSE GROWER

               MINIATURE/PATIO
      White in stock
      Code    Type              Scent    Price
      MP45    Pour Toi          SF       £3.50
      MP142   Cinderella        SF       £2.95
```

```
           *** PRESS 0 FOR LAST MENU ***
```

Page 143

```
           *** ROSEA GARDENS ***
           SPECIALIST ROSE GROWER

              MINIATURE/PATIO
    Reds in stock
    Code     Type               Scent   Price
    MP88     Scarlet Gem        SF      £2.95
    MP124    Little Buckeroo    SF      £3.25

         *** PRESS 0 FOR LAST MENU ***
```

GLOSSARY OF TERMS

Absolute	When used with the replication function in a spreadsheet, it means that where two cells are linked with a formula (A1*b1), the actual formula in that cell is used throughout the replication process, unlike the *relative replication* whereby each cell number is automatically adjusted.
Access	To get data from a computer or call up a file.
Acoustic coupler	A type of modem which provides the means to transmit computer data over telephone lines.
Acoustic hood	A printer cover or hood which reduces noise when printing.
A4	An international size sheet of paper used for typing or word processing.
Align	When figures are required to line up under a decimal point or when paragraphs require reformatting.
Alphanumeric	A set of characters made up of both letters and numbers, e.g. for use in a database.
Background	Operations carried out leaving the screen to be used as normal, e.g. printing from disk.
Backup	A copy: to backup a disk means to copy the information to another disk.
Block	A term used to describe a portion of text, i.e. a sentence or paragraph.
Boilerplating	Whereby blocks of text can be stored and recalled in order to build a document, e.g. standard paragraphs.
Bold/embolden	A word processing text-enhancement feature which emphasises text by printing it in a darker print.
Buffer	An area of memory between parts of a computer storing information sent from one part to the other, e.g. computer and printer.
Cell	The square into which text, numbers or formulae are entered.
Centring	A word processing function which enables text to be positioned in the centre of the screen or between the margins on hard copy.
Column	A number of squares (cells) positioned vertically on the screen.
Condition	Defining a specific fact about data in a field, e.g. 'Is the colour red?' or 'Is the number greater than another number?'
Cursor	The small flashing square or dash on a screen which indicates where commands will affect the text, or where new text keyed in will appear.
Cut and paste	A word processing facility whereby a block of text can be taken from one file (CUT) and moved into another file (PASTE).
Daisywheel	The name given to a type of printer which has the print head shaped like a daisy with the characters positioned on each petal.
Data	Information which is fed into a computer. Data becomes useful information when the computer processes and sorts it into meaningful form.
Database	A large file or pool of information organised in such a way that it can be easily retrieved in a specific form.
Dedicated	A name given to a word processor which is capable of word processing only unlike a PC on which a word processing package can be loaded.
Delete	Remove text and the spaces it took up.

Disk	The most common storage medium in computing – can be either rigid (hard disk) or flexible (floppy).
Diskette	Another name for a floppy disk.
Dot matrix	A name given to a type of printer whereby print is achieved through a series of dots.
Edit	Recall a document and add to it or make alterations to it.
Elite	Text printed 12 characters to the inch.
Erase	When text is removed but the spaces are left.
Fax	Facsimile transmission means sending printed or handwritten documents down a telephone line.
Field	Part of a record containing one piece of information e.g. a name or telephone number.
File	Structured collection of records.
Footer	When a word or words are commanded to repeat on the bottom of every page.
Format	Prepare disk for storage of information; it can also mean the layout of text in word processing.
Frame	A single screen-sized picture of videotexed information or desktop publishing, a portion of a page set aside.
Function key	A key which is programmed to do a specific task.
Graphics	Information or data presented in the form of drawings, diagrams or graphs. Some word processing systems can use graphics to draw horizontal and vertical lines.
Global	A command used in spreadsheets and word processing to change something every time it is met within the spreadsheet or document.
Hard copy	Information printed on paper.
Hard disk	A computer storage device, rigid rather than floppy.
Hardware	The parts of a computer system which can be seen.
Header	Text that is commanded to repeat at the top of every page.
Highlighting	When specific text is shown slightly brighter or darker than the rest on screen, e.g. when moving text or emboldening. This is also known as *reverse video*.
Impact	A type of printer in which the printing device (spokes or keys) actually hits the paper through a ribbon.
Index	Another term for disk directory.
Information technology	This includes three technologies: computing, microelectronics and telecommunications whereby information is collected, stored, processed and distributed electronically i.e. by computer.
Ink jet	A method of printing by spraying fine jets of ink onto paper.
Insert	A word processing facility in which existing text is moved over to make room for new text to be added.
Integer	A whole number.
Integrated package	Software using word processing, spreadsheet, database and possibly communication facilities. It has the ability to fully integrate all functions, i.e. call a spreadsheet into word processing and/or use database for mailmerge, etc.
Justify	When the right-hand margin is flush (straight).
Keyboard	A input device in computing.
Laser	A method of printing using laser beams: a very high quality print is achieved.
Letter quality	Another high-level style of print available.
Load	The action of bringing a program or file into the computer's main memory.
Log	LOG ON or LOG OFF: the action of going into or leaving a computer system.
Mailmerge	A word processing facility in which a standard letter file can be merged with an address file to create personalised letters.

Memory	A term used for storage within a computer.
Menu	A list of options listed on the screen, e.g. OPEN, EDIT, SAVE, PRINT. The initial letter is usually all that is required.
Modem	A device enabling data to be sent down a telephone line. A modem converts data into signals for transmission and then converts it back again for the receiving computer to read.
Move	A word processing facility in which text can be moved from one area to another.
Network	A number of computers connected by communication links.
Numeric	Data consisting of numbers only.
Output	Data processed on screen or printed.
Overwriting	The process of updating files, replacing the old version.
Package	A number of software programs.
Page break	An instruction to start a new page, either inserted by the word processor operator or automatically by the machine.
Pagination	When a document is adjusted to give the same page length throughout.
PC	Personal computer.
Password	For security reasons a computer program may request a password before allowing entry to unauthorised persons.
Peripherals	Equipment designed to work with a computer, i.e. printer.
Pica	Text printed 10 characters to the inch.
Printers	Output devices.
Program	A list of instructions to a computer.
Prompts	Messages which appear on screen to help the user.
Qwerty	A standard typewriter keyboard.
RAM	Random Access Memory.
Range	An area of the spreadsheet, i.e. a number of rows/columns or cells.
Recall	Open or call up an existing file.
Record	Data pertaining to the same person or thing organised into fields.
Relative	When the formulae and contents of a cell change adjusting to fit the row and column numbers.
Replicate	To repeat the same formulae in other cells.
Reverse video	Another name for *highlighting* text.
ROM	Read Only Memory.
Row	A number of squares (cells) positioned horizontally on the screen.
Scroll	The action of moving through a document from start to finish because only a small part of the document is visible on screen at any one time.
Search	Looking for specific data in a database file.
Search and replace	A word processing facility in which a search can be made throughout a document for specific word(s) and other word(s) inserted instead.
Sector	A portion of a disk.
Shared logic	A configuration of terminals which use the same central processing unit.
Shared resource	A configuration of computers possibly sharing the same printer.
Shift key	A key which when pressed in conjunction with another key normally produces CAPITALS or alternative character.
Soft copy	Information on the screen which has yet to be printed.
Sort	Where the data is organised into a specific order, e.g. alphabetical or numerical.
Spreadsheet	A computer program which allows text and numbers to be stored in a grid of rows and columns and used for calculation.

Stand-alone	A computer which has its own central processing unit and does not need to be connected to any other source of computing, e.g. a PC.
Status line	A line displayed on the screen containing information about the current state of affairs, e.g. which line, page and document is being displayed.
String	A number of characters or words.
Subscript	A character printed below the normal print line.
Superscript	A character printed above the normal print line.
Switch code	A code embedded with the text, usually when merging files.
Teletext	An information service offered by TV companies.
Terminal	An input/output device attached to a computer, usually made up of a keyboard and screen, sometimes known as a workstation.
Textname	A name given to a file.
Tractor feed	A name given to a printer device in which sprockets hold the computer printout paper with perforated edges.
Transmission	The act of sending information from one location to another.
Tree structure	The way in which data is stored i.e. in viewdata systems.
Update	Saving a new version of the file once additions or corrections have been made during editing.
Variables	A named item within a spreadsheet or in word processing which can be given a set of values, e.g. a variable in mailmerge can be an address.
VDU	Visual Display Unit (screen).
Videotex	The general name for information services provided on a screen, e.g. viewdata and teletext.
Viewdata	Two-way communicating information service, e.g. Prestel.
Virus	A fault or bug in a computer system which can be passed from one system to another.
Volatile	Capable of being lost: for example volatile memory is lost when the computer is shut off.
Widows and orphans	The last line of a paragraph printed on a new page; the first line of a new paragraph printed on the previous page.
Windows	Split screens whereby different files can be viewed on screen at the same time.
Word processor	A computer application to process text quickly.
Wraparound	Term used to describe word processing feature in which text which is too long to fit on a line is automatically taken to the beginning of the next line.
Write	The act of recording information on disk.
Write protect	A means of protecting data: a small tab can be placed over the notch on a disk, preventing overwriting of information on that disk.
WYSIWYG	An acronym for *What You See Is What You Get*, used by word processor manufacturers: in other words the screen layout is exactly what will be printed.